Frank Sinatra
at the Movies

By the same author

James Stewart: The Hollywood Years

Frank Sinatra
at the Movies

ROY PICKARD

ROBERT HALE · LONDON

ISBN 0 7090 5105 0

Robert Hale Limited
Clerkenwell House
Clerkenwell Green
London EC1R 0HT

2   4   6   8   10   9   7   5   3   1

Photoset in Ehrhardt by
Derek Doyle & Associates, Mold, Clwyd.
Printed in Great Britain by
St Edmundsbury Press Ltd, Bury St Edmunds, Suffolk.
Bound by WBC Ltd, Bridgend, Mid-Glamorgan.

Contents

Illustrations

7

PICTURE CREDITS

The illustrations in this book come from the stills issued to publicize films made or distributed by the following companies.

RKO: 1. MGM: 2, 3, 4, 10, 11, 14. Universal: 5. Columbia: 6, 7, 17. Warner Brothers: 8, 21. United Artists: 9, 12, 13, 18, 19, 20. Goldwyn: 15. Paramount: 16, 22. 20th Century Fox: 23, 24, 25.

Introduction

In many ways, Frank Sinatra as an actor is more exciting than his films. His work – which is, at best, immensely impressive – speaks for itself, and it raises two major questions: Was he really as good as they said he was? And was his film career as much of a roller-coaster ride as has been painted – up one minute, down the next, full of frictions, rows, explosions, tantrums, studio battles and stormy relationships?

The answer to both is 'yes' and this book attempts to reflect some of the speed and frenetic pace of that roller-coaster ride as Sinatra moved swiftly from one major studio to the next, climbing from humble beginnings at RKO to become one of the most powerful men in Hollywood.

He made fifty-nine movies, just a third of them musicals. His work includes such successes as *On The Town*, *From Here to Eternity*, *The Man With The Golden Arm* and *The Manchurian Candidate*. It also encompasses expensive flops, forgettable jobs for hire and home movies he made with 'The Clan'. But although it includes failures it never includes pretentious failures. All of Sinatra's films were aimed at the mass audience. Even when making his most ambitious pictures he never forgot that movies were for the millions, not the thousands.

No one who has had anything to do with the movie business is impartial about Sinatra. He is inherently fascinating. In Hollywood, his pugnacious, happy-go-lucky, chip-on-the-shoulder personality carried all before him. Director Gordon Douglas, who guided him through more films than any other, called him 'the king, one of the most exciting performers in all of show business'. It is difficult to disagree. Perfection in any art form is rare but Sinatra singing Cole Porter's 'I've Got You

Under My Skin' backed by an orchestra conducted by Nelson Riddle, comes close. It is three minutes of poetry in motion.

That though is his musical side. This book deals with his other side, his acting talent. Did he achieve on screen anything remotely comparable to those three minutes of 'I've Got You Under My Skin'? Many who worked with him believed that he did and it is to those directors and fellow workers, songwriters and composers who gave of their time to recall some of those great moments as well as unique anecdotes and behind-the-scenes stories that I offer my gratitude. I could not have compiled this book without them.

This then is the story of the screen Sinatra, a story which began with his birth on 12 December 1915 in Hoboken, New Jersey, and which continued through his teens as he vowed to follow in the footsteps of his idol Bing Crosby. In 1931 Crosby had made crooning popular with his own radio show and, as a result, landed a profitable contract at Paramount Studios in Hollywood. Sinatra was determined to do the same.

At first, movies held no interest for him. It was only the music that mattered. He sang at high school, with orchestras, at school dances – with just about anyone who would have him. Eventually, he progressed to working as a professional, or, as he liked to put it, 'as an amateur but getting paid'. His first break came when Harry James offered him a job as his band's vocalist. After that came Tommy Dorsey and he was on his way.

His long-time girlfriend Nancy Barbato travelled with him on the road and helped him through the lean times. They married in February 1939 and a year later she bore him the first of their three children, Nancy, jun.

His biggest gamble came when he decided to go solo. Close colleagues warned him against it. Too risky, they said. His voice was too light. He ignored them. He was still after Crosby's crown. 'I thought maybe that people were ready for a new kind of singer,' he said later. 'I also thought that I'd better give it a go as quickly as I could. There were singers with other orchestras who were much better than I was. If they'd have gone out before me they would have made it tougher for me to make a mark.'

Agent George Evans made sure he made his mark. In December 1942 he hired thousands of girls to fill the Paramount Theatre in New York and shriek and scream and swoon the minute Sinatra set foot on the stage. 'What the hell was that?' exclaimed a visibly shaken Benny Goodman who was conducting the orchestra when he heard the crescendo of sound.

'That' was the arrival of 'The Voice' as the 27-year-old Sinatra had been named. Young bobbysoxers (so called because of the ankle socks they always wore) went into peals of ecstasy whenever he sang a note or moved a muscle. He was so good they would probably have screamed anyway but Evans wasn't taking anything for granted. He achieved his aim. Sinatra made the front pages. Less than a year later he was on his way to Hollywood.

He had been there before, briefly, as a vocalist with Tommy Dorsey, doing one-song guest spots in a trio of forgettable movies: *Las Vegas Nights, Ship Ahoy* and *Reveille With Beverly*. The work on each lasted for no more than a day. A couple of days later he was back on the road with Dorsey. Now it was for real. He bade a temporary farewell to his two Nancys and settled back in his seat on the luxury train, The Santa Fe Chief. He hadn't any idea as to how things would turn out but if anyone had told him that he would be making movies for the next forty years it is doubtful whether he would have believed them.

Acknowledgements

The interviews included in this book were conducted in Hollywood, New York and London. I am grateful to all of those who talked so freely and enthusiastically about Sinatra in Hollywood and the studio system in which he worked. My thanks go especially to George Axelrod, Sammy Cahn, Frank Capra, Saul Chaplin, Lee J. Cobb, Richard Condon, Ken Darby, John Frankenheimer, Johnny Green, Ray Heindorf, Elia Kazan, Lewis Milestone, Vincente Minnelli, Lee Remick, Debbie Reynolds, Nelson Riddle, George Sidney, Jule Styne, Charles Walters and Fred Zinnemann.

1 RKO

'This is the dopiest thing I've ever had to
do in my life.'

Frank Sinatra

It was director Tim Whelan who drew the short straw. As Sinatra sped across country by train towards RKO, the film-maker was called to the front office. Studio boss Charles Koerner broke the news. He smiled and said, 'Tim, you've got the studio's prize assignment of the year.' Whelan's heart sank. He'd got Sinatra. The other directors on the lot relaxed.

The unwritten law among film-makers, just as it was among actors, was that you never worked with children and you never worked with animals. And if, by some unlucky twist of fate, you found yourself working with both, you contemplated suicide. There was also a third rule: you avoided singers who knew absolutely nothing about acting or film-making. Whelan awaited Sinatra with trepidation.

The mood of Sinatra's West Coast fans was much more enthusiastic. They couldn't wait to get a glimpse of their idol. When he alighted at Pasadena railway station in August of 1943 they were in ecstatic mood. Nearly 6,000 of them besieged the platform. Sinatra was pinned against the coaches, unable to free himself for nearly twenty minutes as fans and autograph hunters fought to catch a glimpse of 'Frankie'. Disgruntled reporters, most of whom didn't want to be there in the first place, were brushed aside. One was bitten on the forearm by a girl determined to get a closer look at Frank. 'Why the hell can't you grow up!' he shouted.

'What do *you* know about it?' she screamed back. 'He's ours, he's ours. *You're* the one who shouldn't be here!'

Agent George Evans brushed aside the accusation that he'd stage-managed the whole thing. He told those reporters who had survived the fraças that it had been a last-minute decision to leave the train at Pasadena. Sinatra had originally intended to go on to Los Angeles station. A rueful journalist, checking carefully for scars and bruises, didn't believe him. He asked why the loudspeaker at the station had been blaring out the Sinatra hit, 'All or Nothing At All' when the train had pulled into Pasadena. Evans just smiled.

Sinatra had been brought to RKO to help bring a new look to the studio. New boss Koerner was determined to get away from the prestige productions of his predecessor, George Schaefer. All Schaefer's policy had produced were a couple of masterpieces by Orson Welles, *Citizen Kane* and *The Magnificent Ambersons*, and near bankruptcy. Koerner wanted none of that. The studio had been down that route once before in the thirties when the musicals of Astaire and Rogers had saved the day. Now, Koerner believed that audience pictures would do the same. The war was on. Anything that had songs in it would sell. The army wanted musical entertainment. It didn't matter about the story, just as long as the songs were good.

Koerner knew he had a lot of ground to make up. RKO was not the most glamorous of Hollywood watering holes. It was a long way down the unofficial league table of leading studios. MGM was top of the heap, *the* great big studio of the great big studios. Then came Paramount in second place, followed by Warner, 20th Century Fox and Harry Cohn's Columbia. RKO nudged in at number six, just ahead of Universal. After that came Republic. Disney was still producing only animated features and cartoon shorts and was not up with the majors.

All things considered, Sinatra's terms were not ungenerous: $25,000 for the first film which would be titled *Higher And Higher*, $50,000 for the second and $100,000 for the third. In return for his outlay Koerner wanted healthy profits and films that would rid the studio once and for all of the amusing but cruel joke that had been circulating around Hollywood during the previous couple of years: 'In case of an air raid make for RKO. They haven't had a hit in years.'

14

Director Tim Whelan was pleasantly surprised by Sinatra. All his fears proved unjustified. The singer was pleasant, a little on the nervous side and at times surprisingly shy in front of the cameras. He was also frequently embarrassed. When he was required to play a scene in which he had to knock on a door whilst carrying a bunch of flowers he broke up in helpless laughter. 'This is the dopiest thing I've ever had to do in my life,' he grinned.

Whelan had been in the business for nearly a quarter of a century. 'Just wait until you hear about some of the things *I've* had to do, Frank,' he offered by way of solace.

The two men got along. Sinatra was a quick learner. Whelan appreciated that. It cut down rehearsal time by half. And for all his initial uncertainty, Sinatra possessed the one essential ingredient necessary to make it in movies – an easy, natural and relaxed manner in front of the cameras. No amount of acting lessons could give a performer that. You either had it or you didn't. Sinatra had it. Whelan was aware of that after just a week's shooting. His star could even utter trite dialogue (and there was plenty of that in *Higher And Higher*) and get away with it, or at least make it sound more convincing than it actually was.

The only problem was Sinatra's impatience. He bored quickly. He couldn't keep still on set. If there was a delay in filming he would get snappy. He was used to rapid work on radio and with dance bands. His restlessness affected his fellow workers especially when he found it difficult to keep his temper between set-ups.

Once, after completing a musical number with Mel Torme and Marcy McGuire, he turned on his heel, left the set and headed straight for his dressing-room. McGuire was especially upset. She was a Sinatra fan. She had been hoping for a word of encouragement. It was not Sinatra's way. He detested hanging around on set. He much preferred to wait in his dressing room where he could make telephone calls, close deals, book concerts. As Mel Torme later reflected, 'Even then, on his first film, he was wheeling and dealing and performing and acting for something like twenty-four hours a day. The demands on his time were quite staggering.'

There was also the entourage. His agent, publicity men, record executives and others were with him all the time. He was

15

never alone. Neither did he want to be alone. He was always busy. One of his co-stars, French actress Michèle Morgan, said, 'The entourage was always in the way of very much personal contact. We did get to know each other a bit and he was friendly when we did get the chance to talk but unlike the rest of us on the film there was always something happening to him. He was never still, not for a moment.'

Sinatra's role in *Higher And Higher* was that of a wealthy young man living next door to a household of servants attempting to pass off their French maid as an heiress. As well as Morgan, his co-stars included Leon Errol, Victor Borge and Dooley Wilson who played the piano just as he had done a year earlier in *Casablanca*. The film derived from a Rodgers and Hart musical that had flopped on Broadway. Rodgers and Hart had not been at their best so RKO brought in Jimmy McHugh and Harold Adamson to write some new numbers. Sinatra got to sing five of them including the memorable 'It's A Lovely Way To Spend An Evening'.

When it came to recording the songs for the movie, Whelan handed over responsibility to musical director Ken Darby whose job it was to explain to Sinatra just how they went about recording on film. Darby knew that Sinatra had always sung in front of a band with just the one mike. It had been that way ever since he had started with Harry James. He had known nothing else. In the studio it was different. Darby recalled:

> On the first day of recording I said, 'Frank, I want to show you something. We'll record the song in two ways, first your way with you standing next to the conductor, then my way. He said, 'What's your way?' I said, 'Well, it's this, you go over to that booth and you do it over again so that we can experiment with something in the control room upstairs, in the mixing room.'
>
> Anyway, we did it, first in front of the orchestra then again in the booth. He did a beautiful recording the first time, he really tried, and an even more beautiful recording with the second one. Then I took him up to the mixing room. I gave him the knobs for the orchestra in one hand and the knobs for his voice in the other. I said, 'Now see what you can do.' Well, he pulled the orchestra out and of course it was there with his voice. He did the same with his voice and again the orchestra was always there. He couldn't do anything with either. He couldn't reduce the

orchestra to let himself stand out a little bit and he couldn't build himself up on the orchestra mike.

Then we put on the other one and he saw he could mix himself into the orchestra exactly the way he wanted to. That sold him. From then on, there was no question. He did it on separate tracks.

As Sinatra would later remark, however, he was not completely sold on the idea. He had reservations about the method right through his movie career. He would have much preferred to have gone on set and recorded the whole thing without any mixing at all. 'I never sing a song the same way twice,' he grumbled. 'I can never understand why, with all this modern technology, they can't record a song on set and get it perfect the first time round. It would sound more natural.'

Higher And Higher was released on 24 January 1944 at the Palace Theatre in New York. The critics who were sharpening their knives to kill off the young crooner and dismiss him as nothing more than an upstart with a bunch of screaming young fanatics in tow had to sheath their weapons. The experience of watching Sinatra on screen was not half as trying as they had imagined. The film itself wasn't much – a here today, gone tomorrow piece of nonsense that was of little consequence. Sinatra though was a different matter. He was not in the usual run of leading men. He was skinny and frail looking and had sunken cheeks. One critic even went so far as to call him ugly. But throughout the film he demonstrated that he was possessed of an interesting screen persona that was waiting to be developed.

The highly regarded *New Yorker* said simply, 'Mr Sinatra comes out fine. He has some acting to do and he does it.' At the other end of the spectrum, the trade paper the *Hollywood Reporter* commented, 'The camera captures an innate shyness in the singer who has uniquely become an idol of the airwaves and the bobby-soxer trade ... people who have never understood his appeal to swooning fans, have even resented him, will have no trouble buying the guy they meet on screen here.'

Bosley Crowther in the *New York Times* led the carpers, 'Frankie is no Gable and no Barrymore. This is a slapdash setting for 'The Voice. It should have been called *Lower And Lower.*'

Somewhere in between these two views was that of John Scott, the critic of the *Los Angeles Times*. He stressed that while Sinatra certainly didn't fulfil the cinema's traditional idea of a romantic figure that should eventually work in his favour. He wrote, 'He appears more at ease than we expected and should find his place as a film personality with careful choice of subjects. Crosby did it, didn't he?'

The last named review gave Sinatra particular pleasure because he was mentioned in the same breath as Crosby. What is more, one of the hit songs written by McHugh and Adamson for the film wound up with an Oscar nomination as one of the best movie songs of 1944. To get on the honours list at your first attempt was a great start by any standards.

The song was called 'I Couldn't Sleep A Wink Last Night'. It didn't win but Sinatra was satisfied just to make the nominations. It would be the first of seven movie songs that would earn him mentions at Oscar time. He was not surprised by the song that won. It came from the Paramount movie *Going My Way*. It was called 'Swinging On A Star'. The composers were James Van Heusen and Johnny Burke. The singer? Bing Crosby.

2   Campaigning for Roosevelt

'It was a mosquito versus a gorilla. Frank
made the score with the sheer force of
his character.'

Orson Welles

Just a fence separated RKO from Paramount. It ran across the
length of the two lots, dividing Crosby, Hope, Lamour, Cooper,
Milland and the others from the somewhat lesser stars at RKO,
most of whom were on their way down or had nowhere to go.
There was a feeling of pride among those who worked at
Paramount. It was not a feeling shared by those employed next
door. At RKO, actors felt very much like also-rans. To the
question, 'Where are you working at the moment?' they would
hurriedly reply, 'Oh, I'm at RKO. It's just a two-picture deal,
nothing more. I've got other things in the pipeline.' No one ever
boasted about working for RKO!

Certainly Sinatra didn't view it as a permanent place of
residence. The people were friendly enough and there was no
pressure as there was at other studios with a mogul cracking the
whip all the time. But it was not exactly where he wanted to be.
His eyes were firmly fixed on that fence. Crosby was only a few
hundred yards away. He was the top money-making star in the
world. He was the top recording artist. There was talk that he
was going to win an Oscar for *Going My Way*. Sinatra wanted to
be Crosby. Movies were somewhat more fun than he'd
imagined. He wanted to be at Paramount or at least somewhere

as good as Paramount. He let his ambitions nurture inside of him.

His main concern in December 1943 was whether any future developments in his career would have to be postponed. His army call-up was imminent. In November he had been passed A-1 at his physical. Induction was set for 1 January. RKO had come to terms with the fact that they would lose their young crooner for the duration and that just a single movie was all they were going to get from their young star, at least for the time being. Then came news of another physical. The press wondered openly why there was a need for a second one. It was held on 9 December at the Newark Induction Centre. The physical examination took one hour and fifteen minutes.

'I can tell you it wasn't an ordeal,' said Sinatra to the waiting press as he left the Centre. 'But I found out a lot of things about myself that I didn't know and a few things I'd better take care of right away.'

He looked heavy-eyed and weary as he issued his statement. The night before, he'd 'knocked 'em dead' at a packed movie-house in Boston where teenagers had again screamed their lungs out for a sight and sound of Frankie. He'd travelled through the night to attend the physical. The doctors had told him he had a hole in his left eardrum which had probably been caused by a series of mastoid operations he'd undergone between the ages of three and seven years.

The doctors' verdict meant that Sinatra would not be serving in the Armed Forces. His file went from Newark to Fort Jay in New York and then to Washington. Officials checked over the papers. He was rated 4-F, a classification that was later changed to 2-A which put more simply meant that he was employed in work that was essential to the national health and interest. In other words, he was more use to the Allies with his voice than he was with a rifle. It had been a curious 'will he, won't he' situation. A month earlier he had been passed A-1. Now he was 2-A. Sinatra, it seemed, had gone through so many classifications that no one quite knew what he was.

Charles Koerner was delighted and immediately set up RKO vehicle number two. It was called *Step Lively* and was a version of an old Marx Brothers comedy *Room Service*. Sinatra featured as a playwright with a swoon-worthy voice who takes over the lead in a revue producer's show and turns it into a hit. The film was basically nothing more than an excuse to allow Sinatra to sing. Jule Styne and Sammy Cahn wrote the songs.

The one man not exactly delighted with the news that Sinatra was ready to go with a second movie was Tim Whelan. He and Sinatra had got on fine during *Higher And Higher*. Whelan felt though that he had served his penance. This time perhaps another director could take over and he could move on to something else? 'But Tim, what are you thinking of,' exclaimed Koerner. 'You did such a good job with Frank on *Higher And Higher*. It must be you. He trusts you. You get along. It's a good assignment.'

Whelan had other views. He'd worked as a gag man for Harold Lloyd in the silent days. He'd also been a stage actor and during the thirties had spent much of his time in Britain working for Alexander Korda. He'd directed such stars as Olivier and Ralph Richardson in *Q Planes* and Vivien Leigh and Charles Laughton in *St Martin's Lane*. He'd also put the finishing touches, mainly to the action sequences, to the spectacular *The Thief Of Bagdad*. He'd enjoyed Britain. He liked the atmosphere. The war had driven him back to the States. If *Step Lively* was to be his reward he might just as well be back in Britain, bombs and all. His past accomplishments flashed momentarily through his mind then disappeared. He accepted the assignment. Work was work.

He guided Sinatra through his first 'screen kiss', waiting patiently as the publicity guys and *Look* magazine made the most of it, he put up with a Sinatra temper tantrum when the singer stalked off the set because his leading lady, Gloria DeHaven, was too tall ('Make her take that damned hat off,' snapped Sinatra), and he even endured a day when the *Step Lively* set was shut down completely because secretaries at the studio deserted their desks to nip over to watch Frank at work. Autographs were signed in abundance. Squeals were heard all over the lot. Little work was done on the movie. Secretaries were thereafter forbidden to leave their desks on any future occasion.

On the final day of shooting, Whelan and Sinatra shook hands. 'No hard feelings, Frank,' said Whelan. 'But that's as far as I go with musicals. If I hear another squeal or shriek or bobby-soxer or anything to do with crooning I think I'll go mad.'

He grinned at Sinatra. 'You're going to be a fine actor some day. I hope I'm around to see it when it happens.'

In every way, 1944 was a very good year for Sinatra. His wife, Nancy, gave birth to their second child, Frank, jun., he had the most popular coast-to-coast radio show on the air, and RKO offered him a long-term contract which he accepted in the hope that one of the bigger studios might eventually pick him up. He noticed that Fox had just gone for singer Dick Haymes. Perhaps Paramount or Warners or Metro might show an interest in him? A long shot but he allowed the thought to cross his mind.

Socially too he enjoyed himself. He had his own gambling entourage. They went to the fights, the track, Palm Springs, Las Vegas and to all of Frank's singing engagements. At weekends they formed a softball team called 'The Swooners' and played at Beverly Hills High School. Regulars included Frank, songwriters Jule Styne and Sammy Cahn, and actors Anthony Quinn and Barry Sullivan. The cheer-leaders, all of them wearing swooner T-shirts, were Virginia Mayo, Marilyn Maxwell, Lana Turner and Ava Gardner. The last three ladies would come to know Frank very well indeed by the time the decade had come to an end. As the press would note with increasing regularity, Sinatra was not impervious to the attractions of Hollywood beauty.

The year was also important to Sinatra for a much more serious reason. It marked the first time he became actively involved in politics. As Franklin Roosevelt began campaigning for an unprecedented fourth term, Sinatra came out firmly for the President and immediately instigated the wrath of the right-wing press. In the eyes of the powerful Republican press he became a marked man.

Sinatra said later, 'My first real criticism from the press came when I campaigned for President Roosevelt in 1944. I felt it was the duty of every American citizen to help elect the candidate of his choice. Ginger Rogers, George Murphy and other stars supported the Republican Tom Dewey during the campaign. I noticed that none of my critics lambasted them.'

In 1944 Sinatra's stance was a brave one. Only a handful of names in the movie world went public regarding their politics. Compared to the eighties and nineties when Warren Beatty, Paul Newman, Shirley MacLaine, Robert Redford, Barbra

Streisand and others showed themselves to be politically conscious, most Hollywood stars kept their political affiliations to themselves. Very few came out openly in support of a candidate.

Frank's daughter Nancy recalled that in 1944 a famous comedian had agreed to broadcast for Roosevelt but was urged by friends and advisers to think again. What if Roosevelt should lose, they argued. People who had been the comedian's fans might desert him if they had made up their minds to vote the other way. They could resent him for his stand. His pictures and his personal appearances might do bad business. His income could be halved. Was it worth it? The comedian thought not. He withdrew from the broadcast.

Sinatra had no such qualms. He deliberately went for a high profile. He laid his views on the line at rallies and on TV and radio. He campaigned right across the country. If his fans differed from his politics then so be it. That was their affair just as campaigning for Roosevelt was his.

His interest in politics was nothing new. As a boy he had been influenced by his mother. She had busied herself with the welfare of unmarried mothers in Hoboken, New Jersey, where intolerance, racial prejudice and bigotry were never far from the surface. As an Italian-American he had received his own share of abuse and jeers of 'wop' and 'dago'. His early years had taught him to stand up for minority groups and the little guy. His whole background made him a natural democrat.

Orson Welles, one of Frank's earliest acquaintances in Hollywood and a fellow supporter of Roosevelt, witnessed at first hand Sinatra's volatility on the campaign trail. During the tub-thumping he and Sinatra found themselves sharing a car on the way to a rally. When they pulled up at a roadside diner for a coffee they asked their driver to join them. The driver was black. The man in the diner took one look and asked the driver to leave. Sinatra leaned across and grabbed the man by his shirt front. According to Welles the man was a giant. It made no difference to Sinatra. He said, 'You're serving coffee for *three*!' The barman hesitated but not for long. Remembered Welles, 'There was no sporting event there. It was a mosquito versus a gorilla. Frank made the score with the sheer force of his character.'

Sinatra was no stranger to such incidents. During the early dance band days he'd harangued a hotel clerk for refusing to admit a black musician for the night. 'It's OK, Frank,' said the jazzman, anxious to let it go, 'I'm used to it.'

'Well, I'm not,' said Sinatra. He turned to the clerk.

'It's not our policy ... ' began the employee.

'I don't give a damn about your policy. Is this guy staying here or not?' The jazzman was admitted. On another occasion, during a Dorsey date, Sinatra attacked a member of the audience for making anti-Semitic remarks. He refused to continue until the man was silenced.

The irritation of the right-wing press with Sinatra reached its peak when Frank was invited to have tea with Roosevelt at the White House. It was a clever move by the wise and crafty president. Sinatra was at the peak of his popularity. He was just about to enjoy another huge success at the Paramount in New York where more than 25,000 screaming teenagers would line the streets just to get a glimpse of their idol. As a publicity stunt to attract the young vote, Sinatra's White House visit was a stroke of genius.

For Sinatra, publicity gimmick or not, it was the fulfilment of a lifetime's ambition. 'He's the greatest guy alive,' he said of Roosevelt. Later, having chipped in $5,000 at a rally in Madison Square Garden, he told the audience, 'He is good for me and my kids and my country.' On his radio broadcasts he presented himself as 'a little guy from Hoboken'.

Right-wing journalist Westbrook Pegler preferred to refer to him as 'The Hoboken 4-F'. He stirred up as much trouble for Sinatra as he could and even raised an old issue of Sinatra being arrested (and eventually exonerated) on a morals charge in the thirties.

Pegler was a long time critic of Roosevelt's New Deal. He also disliked Sinatra. He had him tagged as a philanderer and a troublemaker. Sinatra made a mental note not to forget Pegler's vicious newspaper attacks.

Shortly after Roosevelt's re-election he noticed Pegler in the Wedgwood Room at the Waldorf Astoria where Sinatra was appearing for a singing engagement. It was the late show. Sinatra saw red, 'Get that bum out of here or I don't perform,' he told the manager.

The manager was helpless. He told Sinatra that he couldn't do that. 'Don't mess with Pegler, Frank,' said George Evans. 'Just let it go. He's too powerful.'

Sinatra refused to budge. He'd get the bum out of there if it was the last thing he did. He instructed one of his aides to leave the room and fake a long-distance telephone call for the columnist. The call was timed for two minutes before the show was due to start. Pegler was paged. Seconds after he left the room Sinatra stepped up to the microphone and began to sing. The house rule was that, once the show had started, no one could be seated. Pegler was refused re-admission. There was a smile in Sinatra's voice as he watched Pegler retreat with his tail between his legs.

No one was refused admission to *Step Lively* when it was released in July of 1944. The fans came in their thousands. Cinema managers viewed the avalanche with a new kind of dread. Stills would be torn from front-of-house displays, lipstick smudged across the posters and the seats inside almost wrenched from their hinges. During live performances some teenagers were so overcome they not only screamed and fainted they also wet themselves. They did the same in movie-houses across the country. The cleaners, even more than the managers, were glad when a Sinatra movie had completed its run.

One critic, Arch Winsten of the *New York Post*, actually had the courage to watch the movie with an audience rather than at the usual press screening. He complained that the Sinatra swoon and squeal society was in force at the Palace Theatre and that he hadn't always been able to pay attention to the picture. He added, 'Whenever Mr Sinatra does anything the slightest bit endearing his followers let forth such an ear-piercing shriek that further calm judgment is out of the question. This is usually followed by loud noises from sailors and others pretending to excess masculinity. The result is a portion of bedlam.'

Sinatra was at his peak of popularity in 1944. He was idolized from coast to coast. Nothing could dent the ardour of his fans two of whom made their way to Frank's Californian home determined to claim something of his for their own. On arrival they pleaded with Nancy to give them a pair of Frank's shorts that were hanging from the clothes line. Nancy declined the request. The bobbysoxers refused to give up. They eyed the safety pin that was holding the shorts on the line. They looked at Nancy. How about the pin? Nancy took pity. The girls went home waving the safety pin in the air. They were the envy of every teenager they met.

3 MGM and L.B. Mayer

'He didn't fall off the horse, he fell off
Ginny Simms.'

Frank Sinatra

Louis B. Mayer wept unashamedly. He was with his wife at a
Hollywood Benefit for a home for the Jewish aged. Frank
Sinatra was the man causing the tears. He was singing the
Jerome Kern classic 'Ol Man River'. Mayer nudged his aide
Eddie Mannix and said, 'I want that boy at Metro.'

Mannix passed him a handkerchief and said, 'RKO have him.
He's under contract.'

'Buy it out!'

Suddenly Sinatra was an MGM star! From the start he was
L.B.'s boy. Mayer was like a father, Sinatra was like a son. Other
stars on the lot would josh him about his special privileges.
Gene Kelly, Judy Garland, Kathryn Grayson, Van Johnson, all
of them, would chide, 'Here comes the *star* – and what did Mr
Mayer do for you today?'

The answer was really not much more than he'd done for any
of them when they'd first arrived at the studio. Mayer liked to
father everyone at Metro. The entire lot was his family. If
anyone had problems he liked to hear about them. He would
take care of everything. Their welfare was his concern. Nothing
was too much trouble. Except when they asked for a raise in
salary. Then it was a different matter.

Negotiations over Sinatra's contract were long and
protracted. They took fully three months. Sinatra's terms were
that he be allowed to make at least one picture outside Metro

27

every year. MGM agreed. He also requested that he make sixteen guest appearances on the radio. Again, MGM went along with his demands just as they did when he asked for publishing rights in music. Sinatra wanted those in alternate films. The end result was a five-year contract at $260,000 a year. MGM believed they had made a wise investment. They had kept a sharp eye on record sales during the negotiations. In 1946 Sinatra's records were selling at a rate of 10 million a year.

At first Metro seemed like heaven to Sinatra. Compared with the cramped facilities at RKO, the Culver City lot was airy and spacious. Instead of a few dozen extras roaming the place, MGM was full to overflowing with stars and character actors, top producers and established directors. In the commissary, performers dressed as politicians, farmers, ballerinas and private-eyes brushed with those attired for exotic dance routines who, in turn, found themselves lunching with soldiers in uniform and elegant Victorian ladies. Gable was back at the studio after wartime service. So too were Robert Taylor and Robert Montgomery. Everything was busy and on the up. Sinatra was part of it all. The mood was infectious.

That he was now actually working at the Rolls-Royce of Hollywood studios really came home to Sinatra when he saw the size of his dressing-room. He'd heard stories that Metro's facilities were luxurious. The stories were not exaggerated. The rooms were large and elegantly designed with wood surrounds made entirely of cedar. Comfortable chairs and settees lined the walls. A coffee-maker was always to hand. So too was a record-player. A deep thick carpet stretched from wall to wall. The only thing missing was a telephone. Mayer felt they were too distracting, especially if stars were learning lines and going over their roles with directors. Sinatra couldn't live without a telephone. Mayer ordered that he receive one immediately. He gave instructions, however, that the phone should not ring. Whenever an incoming call was scheduled, a red light would show above the phone. That way, no one would be disturbed.

The man who was charged by Mayer to 'make something' of Sinatra was producer Arthur Freed, the celebrated head of the studio's musical unit. He found himself in something of a quandary as to what to do with the young crooner. He had viewed the films Sinatra had made at RKO and agreed with most of what the critics had had to say. Sinatra was at ease in front of the cameras. There was no question about that. He also had charm and a slightly impish sense of humour. That showed through as well. And he showed a definite comic potential. Yet, despite all this, he was still basically an inexperienced film performer, a naïve crooner with hollow cheeks and big ears whose neck seemed to disappear into shirts and suits that were generally too large for his skinny frame. There were an awful lot of rough edges still to be smoothed out.

Freed reasoned that if Sinatra was to get anywhere at the studio he needed to dance as well as sing. He turned him over to Gene Kelly, an innovative new star and choreographer who was being talked of as the new Fred Astaire. It was a wise move. Kelly was a man of infinite patience. He took Sinatra under his wing and spent hours gently coaching him in the rudiments of dance and instilling in him the confidence to share the boisterous dance numbers in the musicals Freed was lining up on his schedule. Sinatra never forgot how much he owed Kelly. He said later that Kelly taught him more about movie musicals than anyone in the business. He also remembered, rather ruefully, the length of the rehearsals which often went on for as long as eight weeks, almost the time it took to shoot a whole picture.

Yet, for all Kelly's teaching and kindness, it quickly became apparent to Sinatra that things weren't going as well as they should at Metro. Everything was fine when he was working with Gene. Their pictures made money. He got good notices as the affable foil to the street-smart Kelly in the three pictures they made together. It was when he was without Kelly that he began to realize his limitations.

Within eighteen months it had become depressingly obvious that he couldn't really carry a film on his own. Neither *It Happened In Brooklyn*, a slight tale about a returning GI who finds romance with a young schoolteacher, nor the disastrous *The Kissing Bandit* in which he was ludicrously cast as a romantic outlaw in 1830s Spanish California, did anything for his reputation. A picture he made on loan-out to RKO, *The Miracle Of The Bells*, was another flop, and in the all-star Jerome Kern bio-pic, *Till The Clouds Roll By*, he was no more than a guest star reprising the song that had brought him to Metro in the first place, 'Ol Man River'.

By 1948 disenchantment had set in. In his view he had become little more than a cog in the well-oiled MGM machine, part of a musical formula. The studio saw him basically as a friendly little sailor who sang a few songs, had nothing much to say for himself and generally played second fiddle to his co-stars. Even the joyous *On The Town*, the exhilarating tale of three sailors on a twenty-four-hour shore leave in New York, found him with the most ordinary role, that of the sailor who is constantly on the receiving end of the jokes of wise-cracking cab driver Betty Garrett. Sinatra would later grimace at the memory of his early Metro films and sum up their plots with some embarrassment: 'Kelly and Sinatra meet girl. Kelly hates girl. Sinatra loves girl. Girl likes Sinatra but loves Kelly. Girl rejects Sinatra. Sinatra finds that he loved the first girl all the time. Fade out.'

It was with his songs that Sinatra did best out of the studio. He had insisted that Metro hired Jule Styne and Sammy Cahn for *Anchors Aweigh*. At first, the studio had resisted. Stars did not tell them who to hire and who not to hire. Sinatra, though, was adamant. These guys were good. They knew how to write hit songs. He threatened to walk off the picture unless they were signed. MGM gave in. It was a good move. Sinatra's song 'I Fall In Love Too Easily' was the hit of the picture and swept the country. It also earned Styne and Cahn an Oscar nomination as the best movie song of its year. Two years later the same pair of songwriters did it again when they came up with the wistful 'Time After Time' for *It Happened In Brooklyn*.

Yet even in the song department Sinatra was destined to suffer his disappointments. In the baseball musical *Take Me Out To The Ball Game* he was scheduled to sing the song 'Boys And Girls Like You And Me'. It had been written some ten years earlier by Rodgers and Hammerstein for their musical *Oklahoma!* but had been deleted by the songwriters just prior to the show's opening on Broadway. Arthur Freed was so enamoured with the song that he purchased it for the studio and determined to use it in one of MGM's forthcoming musicals.

Judy Garland was the first choice to sing the number in *Meet Me In St Louis*. At the preview everyone enthused about the song and everyone praised the film. It was just that somehow the two didn't seem to go together. The song sounded as though it had been forced into the film. All the others worked but not 'Boys And Girls Like You And Me'.

Usually, Freed fought for his songs. In 1939 he'd threatened resignation when Mayer wanted to delete 'Over The Rainbow' from *The Wizard Of Oz*. The song's subsequent Academy Award vindicated his decision to fight. On this occasion, however, he bowed to pressure. 'Boys And Girls' was dropped.

Four years later it was Sinatra's turn. Sinatra was delighted and agreed with Freed. It was a fine song. The only mystery was why Rodgers and Hammerstein had cut it from *Oklahoma!* in the first place. Sinatra's rendition was superb. Everyone agreed that the song was the hit of the movie.

Once again the preview proved otherwise. The song was great in its own right but, as far as the picture was concerned, it didn't fit. It was cut. Sinatra was mortified. So too was Freed. 'Boys And Girls Like You And Me' was never heard of again.

The thing that counted most against Sinatra at MGM was his talent for bad publicity. He attracted trouble like a roof conductor attracts lightning. The first thing that displeased Mayer was when he sounded off about the film industry and the people who worked in it. The operative words were 'pictures stink and so do the people who make them'. Many stars and directors made similar comments in the heat of the moment but not when they were within earshot of a journalist who was just a yard or two away interviewing someone else. 'Pictures Stink' inevitably made the headlines. Sinatra duly apologized.

Next came Sinatra's private life. In 1947 he was pictured in Cuba in the company of some mobsters one of whom was Lucky Luciano. The press, especially the right-wing press who had never forgiven him for his efforts on behalf of Roosevelt, began making noises. Was the meeting with Luciano a coincidence? Were there mob connections? What was Sinatra doing in Cuba in the first place?

The photograph was spread right across the front pages. Sinatra protested. He had been on holiday. Someone had introduced them. They had shaken hands. What was he supposed to do, spit in the guy's eye? Agent George Evans went into overdrive to play things down.

On 8 April 1947 the dirt really hit the fan. Sinatra was dining with a group of music business friends at Ciro's on Hollywood's Sunset Strip when a columnist named Lee Mortimer walked in. Like Westbrook Pegler, Mortimer had been anti-Sinatra in the

Roosevelt campaign. In 1945, when Sinatra returned from a seven week tour of Europe and North Africa, Mortimer had sniped in the *New York Daily Mirror*, 'Sinatra waited until hostilities were over in the Mediterranean to take his seven week joy ride, while fragile dolls like Carole Landis and ageing ailing men like Joe E. Brown and Al Jolson subjected themselves to enemy action, jungle disease and the danger of travel through hostile skies from the beginning of the war.' Since then Mortimer had been snapping away at Sinatra's heels for more than two years.

When the two men came face to face in Ciro's words were exchanged. Sinatra threw a punch. Mortimer finished up on the floor. The following afternoon, as he was rehearsing in a radio studio, Sinatra was arrested. He pleaded not guilty to a charge of battery and requested a jury trial. If things went against him he faced a possible jail sentence of six months. Mayer, anxious about the bad publicity for the studio, called him. He advised him to settle. The quicker it was over the sooner it would be forgotten. Sinatra needed some persuasion, even from Mayer. He claimed that it was Mortimer who had provoked him. 'He called me a dago and I saw red.'

'Settle Frank,' said Mayer softly. Sinatra settled. Mortimer received $9000. With all the additional costs Sinatra's payments exceeded $25,000. The proceedings took just six minutes.

None of which went down at all well with L.B. In public he would always be seen to be supporting his stars but in private Sinatra was fast becoming a pain in the neck. A radio poll had just announced that Sinatra was 'The Most Popular Living Person'. Mayer was not one of those who sent in a vote.

The mood of despondency which hung over Sinatra deepened still further when he saw new singers arriving at Metro and being offered prize roles that would soon turn them into major stars. Howard Keel and Mario Lanza were just two who, by 1949, had bright futures ahead of them at the studio. Mayer rolled out the red carpet for both; with Sinatra he simply pulled the rug, and as far as Sinatra was concerned at exactly the wrong time. His records were no longer selling as they once had, his chart songs were struggling to reach number one and bobbysoxers were a thing of the past. The only thing that brightened Sinatra's life was the birth, on 20 June 1948, of his third child and second daughter, Christina, or as she would later become known, Tina.

The beginning of the end for Sinatra at MGM came during the shooting of *On The Town*. Rumours had swept the set that Mayer was going to divorce his wife and that he was dating the singer-actress Ginny Simms. One of Mayer's favourite hobbies was racehorses. He enjoyed gambling on them at the track and riding them at weekends. He was an accomplished horseman but one weekend he found it difficult to handle one especially boisterous steed and was thrown. He finished up with several broken bones. He was in a cast that stretched from his knees to his chest.

The news that Mayer had met with an accident spread quickly round the lot. 'Fatal, I hope,' was the reaction of many employees. Sinatra had his own contribution. He said loudly as he and Gene were preparing for a scene, 'He didn't fall off the horse, he fell off Ginny Simms.'

Those on the *On The Town* set enjoyed the joke. All except Kelly. He raised his eyes and said, 'When are you going to learn to keep your mouth shut you stupid bastard?' Sinatra pulled a 'What the hell it was only a joke' kind of face and forgot all about it.

A few weeks later, when Mayer had recovered, Sinatra got a call that L.B. wanted to see him in his office. 'So, Frank, I hear you've been making jokes about my ladyfriend.' Sinatra felt uncomfortable. Mayer was such a short man that, when he was sitting in his chair behind his desk, his legs dangled and didn't reach the ground. He could be a comical sight when approached from the door of his office. He didn't seem funny now. Mayer smiled and continued, 'That's not a very nice thing to do. So I want you to leave here and I don't ever want you to come back again.' And with that Sinatra was dismissed. He was no longer L.B.'s boy. It had started with Mayer and it had finished with Mayer. His days as a studio contract player were over.

His contract was terminated a year before it was due to expire. MGM agreed to pay him $85,000 in compensation. On 27 April 1950 a joint statement was released announcing Frank's departure, 'As a freelance artist he is now free to accept unlimited important personal appearances radio and television offers that have been made to him.' It sounded impressive but it fooled no one.

Less than two months later, on 17 June 1950, another Metro star – Judy Garland – was let go. She had failed to report for filming on the Fred Astaire musical, *Royal Wedding*. Her contract was suspended. She had been a top star at MGM for more than a decade. Now, at the age of twenty-eight, she was an emotional wreck, a burnt-out case with nothing more to offer. At thirty-four, Sinatra was six years older. The studio had got more than their money's-worth out of Garland; Sinatra though, had been a disappointing investment.

Gene Kelly expressed regret that MGM had let Sinatra go, 'He's the hardest worker I've ever known. I think he's a great singer and has what it takes to make a fine actor. He has a native talent that shows up in his singing and an acting talent that makes you believe what he's doing. I think Metro are foolish to let him go.'

It was with his acknowledgement of Sinatra's *acting* talent that Kelly really got to the truth of the matter. He felt that Metro could have safely taken a chance on him as a dramatic actor. They had nothing to lose. Just one role would have been enough. Many musical stars under contract appeared in the occasional dramatic role between their musical assignments. In 1950 Kelly himself had been cast in a gangster movie called *Black Hand*. He had been chosen simply because he wasn't working on anything at the time. He gave a good account of himself. It would have been worth MGM's while to have tried Sinatra in a similar capacity before they drew a veil over his career at the studio.

There were certainly plenty of opportunities. *Battleground*, the story of the Battle of Bastogne during the last days of the war, was packed with male roles, any one of which Sinatra could have filled. 'B' movies like the boxing drama *Right Cross* also offered possibilities. Then there were comedies like *Three Guys Named Mike*, one of which was played by Howard Keel. If Keel, why not Sinatra? Anything would have been worth a shot but Metro never bothered. All Sinatra had to show for his four years at the studio were a few exuberant dance numbers with Gene Kelly, a couple of hit songs and some enjoyable wisecracking with on-the-make taxi driver Betty Garrett in *On The Town*. The rest was a disappointment.

Many argued that his best cinematic contribution to the

period was made not at MGM but at RKO back in 1945 in a little film called *The House I Live In*. There was no plot to the film. Sinatra (as himself and seen taking a break from a recording session) is pictured talking with some kids who have been chasing another because 'we don't like his religion'. Sinatra calms them down, talks to them about the stupidity of bigotry, remonstrates with them for their attitude and straightens them out. As he goes back to the studio door, one of the boys asks, 'Hey, what do you do for a living?'

Sinatra replies, 'I sing.'

Another says, 'Aw, come on, you're kidding.'

Sinatra answers, 'No, I'll show you,' and sings 'The House I Live In'.

The film was a heartfelt cry against religious and racial intolerance in a society that was only just beginning to recognize and question the dangers of prejudice and bigotry. It was written by Albert Maltz, produced by Frank Ross and directed by Mervyn LeRoy. It was shot in just one day on the RKO lot. Everyone gave their services free. All profits were donated to various juvenile organizations across the country. The film ran for just ten minutes and was distributed to the cinemas without charge. It won a special Academy Award and meant more to Sinatra than anything he subsequently achieved at MGM.

4   Ava

In January of 1950 Ava Gardner accompanied Frank Sinatra to
Houston, Texas, where he was booked to open the new
Shamrock Hotel. A photographer caught sight of them dining
together. Snap! Suddenly, the world knew.

At first Hollywood thought it was more of the same. There
had been affairs before, so many in fact that George Evans's
constant plea to Sinatra was, 'Leave the dames alone Frank.
Think of your marriage and kids, think of your career.' The plea
would fall on deaf ears. Whenever Evans broached the subject
Sinatra's temper would flare. Evans would hold up his hands
and say, 'OK, Frank, OK,' and simply back off.

Lana Turner had been one of the first to make the headlines.
The columnists had given it full play, 'Sinatra and Turner in
Romance! Sinatra plans to leave Nancy and marry me. We are
very much in love.' In the end though, in somewhat smaller print
and usually on an inside page, came the payoff, 'Frank returns to
Nancy and the kids.'

Then Sinatra and Marilyn Maxwell. Big romance. Sinatra
denies his marriage is breaking but Marilyn says this is the real
thing. She and Frank are deeply in love. The columnists pursue
the story further, 'Breakup of marriage imminent!' A few weeks
later he was back to Nancy and the kids.

Next Frank Sinatra and Ava Gardner and this time it is

different, this time it is for real. In Ava's words, 'The first night we made love we became lovers forever, eternally. Big words I know. But I truly felt that no matter what happened we would always be in love. And when we made love that first time, God almighty things did happen.'

Things happened to Louis B. Mayer as well but he didn't enjoy them half as much. The names of Frank and Ava spread across the front pages of newspapers right across the world was bad news for the studio. It sent shock waves through the New York office. The edict came from the top brass, 'Stop it and stop it *now*!' The all-powerful Mayer was under orders.

Mayer had dealt with scandals before. Back in the thirties there had been the controversial death of Jean Harlow and earlier, the grisly suicide of her husband, producer Paul Bern. And there had been any number of occasions when Metro stars had been found drunk and incapable and the police persuaded to keep things out of the papers. But this was different. When it came to morality Hollywood was self-righteous. Stars were supposed to be above reproach. They were idols. Acts of adultery were bad for the image and bad for the industry. Worst of all they were bad for the studio.

Mayer read Ava the riot act. He had known of her infatuation with Sinatra. He had forbidden her to go with Frank to the Shamrock. He did not mince his words, 'You're a whore,' he stormed. 'You were denied permission to leave Los Angeles because I knew what was going on. Have you read the newspapers? Do you know what Hedda and Louella are saying about you? Have you read your fan mail?'

Next he brought up Ingrid Bergman. Just a few months earlier, she too had made the headlines by deserting her husband of twelve years, and also her daughter, and going to live with Italian director Roberto Rossellini whose illegitimate child she was carrying. Such open defiance of ethics and morality had caused an outcry in Hollywood. Again, the name calling had raged for weeks. Bergman, who had just played *Joan Of Arc* on screen, became known as 'Hollywood's apostle of degradation'. Hollywood did not forgive. It would be the mid fifties before Bergman was welcomed back into the fold.

'Look what's happened to Bergman,' snarled Mayer. 'You want to end up like her – finished before you're thirty?' Ava kept calm in the face of Mayer's abuse. She knew he enjoyed his rants. She knew too that he regarded her as one of his major properties. He had just signed her to a ten-year deal for twelve films at $100,000 a picture. It was quite a package especially compared to the paltry pay-off he was about to offer Sinatra to quit the studio. He couldn't afford to lose her over some scandal that might blow over in a couple of months.

He quietened down and brought the familiar father touch into play. He asked if she would end the affair. She shook her head. Would she consider it? Again, no. She waited for the next ploy. Would it be the tears or would it be the morals clause? It was the morals clause.

All stars who signed with studios had the clause inserted in their contracts. The key section read that they should 'conduct themselves with due regard to public conventions and morals and not commit any act or thing that would degrade them in society or bring them into public hatred'. There was more, all of it wrapped in pompous, legalistic jargon, but that was the nub of it.

What it all boiled down to was that stars could do anything in private (and did) providing they didn't get found out. If they happened to slip up in public however, they had to pay the penalty. It was a good job the clause didn't apply to the moguls who ran the studios. If the Mayers, the Warners, the Harry Cohns had been subjected to such a ruling there would have been no moguls, no pictures and no studios. One studio head was known to have no handles on the insides of his office doors as luckless starlets found to their cost once they had trod warily into his inner sanctum.

Bold as she was Ava didn't have the effrontery to mention any of this to L.B. She still needed her job. But she refused to yield to any of his demands. She emphasized again that she and Frank would not give each other up. She knew that she was being depicted as a home-wrecker and Frank as a heel but if the Legion of Decency threatened to ban her movies and Catholic priests wrote her letters condemning her behaviour then so be it. OK, so her mail was being addressed 'Bitch-Jezebel-Gardner' and she was being referred to as 'that scarlet woman'. She could cope with that. She would not stop seeing Frank. That was her final answer. Could she go now? A defeated Mayer threw up his hands and indicated the door. The minute it closed behind her he began making plans to cast her in his all-star Technicolor remake of *Showboat*.

Nancy's reaction to all the scandalous headlines became apparent on St Valentine's Day. A Catholic and reluctant to seek a divorce, she sued instead for separate maintenance. It was granted in September of 1950. Sinatra was instructed to pay her one third of his gross income up to $150,000, then 10 per cent of the gross above that figure until her death or remarriage. The payments were never to fall below $1,000. Nancy would keep the Holmby Hills home, stock in the Sinatra Music Corporation and their 1950 grey Cadillac. She would have custody of the children. Sinatra got to keep his Palm Springs house, a 1949 Cadillac convertible and all his music compositions and records.

All of this would have been enough to ruin just about anyone's year but fate decreed that 1950 was not going to be just any old year for Sinatra. It was going to be the year when *everything* would come crashing down around his ears.

In January he lost through a heart attack his longtime friend and agent, George Evans, the man who had seen him through so many scrapes, both in the movies and the music business. In April, the month he departed from MGM, he opened at the Copacabana in Manhattan only to find in the third show that he could make no sound when he tried to sing. Believing it to be just a false start, he coughed and nodded to the bandleader Skitch Henderson to try again. Nothing. This time he coughed into his handkerchief and this time there was blood. He mumbled a hurried 'goodnight' into the microphone and rushed from the stage. He had suffered a throat haemorrhage. He was away from singing for weeks. 'Nothing came out but dust,' he said later. He was replaced by Billy Eckstine, the singer who had toppled him as the nation's number one vocalist.

Henderson said, 'It was terrifying. I guess the colour drained out of my face as I caught the panic in his. It became so quiet, so intensely quiet in the club. Like they were watching a man walk off a cliff.' Which, to all intents and purposes, they were for just to rub salt in the wounds Columbia informed Sinatra of something of which he was only too well aware. They were having trouble selling his records.

The new man in charge of the Columbia Corporation was

Mitch Miller. He was a man who lacked taste in music. He liked screamers like Frankie Laine and corny numbers like 'Mule Train'. The louder and more vibrant they were so much the better. He had no time for Sinatra's kind of music. To him the slow, wistful ballads and love songs were out of fashion. What's more, he didn't think they would return. He suggested that Sinatra changed his style. He mentioned a couple of songs he might try, 'The Roving Kind' and 'My Heart Cries for You'. Sinatra refused to chase fashion. The songs were recorded by Guy Mitchell and both were hits.

Sinatra didn't have any better luck when he tried television. October saw the launch of his first TV show, a one-hour weekly variety programme that was no different and certainly no better than any of the others being transmitted at the time. It bombed. Sinatra was reportedly impossible to work with, sometimes three hours late for rehearsals and invariably in a mean mood when he did arrive. After thirteen weeks he lost the sponsors and the show.

There were even problems with Ava who was making a picture called *Pandora And The Flying Dutchman* in Spain. The papers carried rumours that Ava was having a fling with a matador named Mario Cabre who was also in the picture. Frank flew to Spain looking for a fight. The bullfighter it turned out was more fond of his own publicity than he was of Ava. She dismissed him as nothing more than a pest.

Sinatra's reversals inevitably brought money troubles in their wake. Always a man who had enjoyed spending freely, he found himself owing more than $200,000 in back taxes. He borrowed the money from Columbia to clear the debt. Forced to accept night-club dates that were not always out of the top drawer and required by law to give Nancy a percentage of everything he earned, he said to Ava ruefully, 'Honey, they're taking me to the cleaners. I don't think I have enough to buy you a pair of nylons.'

Just about the only bright moments of the year occurred in London when he enjoyed a much-needed success at the Palladium. Generally however he was regarded as being the epitome of yesterday's man, a player with virtually no stage to stand upon. It was to stay that way for much longer than he'd anticipated.

5　A Bow-legged Bitch and a Hoboken Bastard!

'Miss Winters and Mr Sinatra do not
speak to each other, so this is the end.'
Agent for Shelley Winters

The grim reality of the situation caught up with Sinatra in 1950. He had no studio and no movies. His records weren't selling. His night-club dates were poorly attended and dwindling. His private life was a mess. Several times he said to Ava, 'I guess I'm right back where I started.'

The only film he thought he might have a chance with was Columbia's version of the William Motley bestseller *Knock On Any Door*. The book was about a slum-bred young hoodlum, Nick 'Pretty Boy' Romano, who is accused of killing a policeman and defended in court by an attorney who himself has successfully graduated from the slums. Humphrey Bogart had been cast as the attorney and Daniel Taradash, later to pen the screenplay for *From Here To Eternity*, had been assigned to write the script. Nicholas Ray was set to direct.

It was the role of the slum kid that intrigued Sinatra. He had known plenty like him when he was a kid himself back in Hoboken. Through his agent he made overtures. Columbia dallied. The prospect was attractive. Bogart and Sinatra. A potent combination. Not, however, quite potent enough. The verdict: Sinatra was thirty-four – he was too old. Sinatra's only defence against that was that he looked younger which indeed he did. Columbia were unimpressed. They gave the role to the

23-year-old newcomer John Derek. For Sinatra it was back to square one and endless months of kicking his heels in frustration as he waited for something to turn up.

It was eighteen months before it did and even then Sinatra felt he was doing little more than clutching at straws. His agent told him there was a part going at Universal. '*Universal!*' exclaimed Sinatra. 'That's no better than RKO!'

'OK, but it's a movie.'

'What is it?'

'*Meet Danny Wilson*. The money's chicken feed. $25,000 but as I say, its a movie. It'll bring you back into the game.'

The film was about a pugnacious young saloon singer who sells a chunk of himself to a night-club racketeer. When he achieves success, the racketeer, now in hiding, wants his percentage. No dice says Sinatra. Aggro all round. Sinatra's girlfriend makes things worse by falling for his pianist accompanist. End result: a shoot-out in a stadium and the death of the racketeer. Girl gets accompanist, Sinatra becomes a star. Final credits. Eighty-five minutes of tosh.

Sinatra hesitated. He wasn't enthralled. What if this one didn't work out? If it died he could be finished for good. At least in movies.

Ava had no doubts. 'Take it,' she said. 'You'll be working again and you'll be in front of the cameras which is what this damned business is all about. You can't be picky.'

Sinatra knew that only too well. He signed for the role, all the time resenting Ava's increasing prominence at Metro, the studio at which he himself had failed to find his niche. Ava's success as the tragic half-caste Julie Laverne in *Showboat* had been especially hard to take. It had not gone unnoticed by the critics, nor by the public, nor by Frank. Her success, especially in a musical, often stretched their relationship to breaking point.

To take some of the tension out of the situation Ava made sure that when she and Frank attended the première of *Showboat* and she was besieged by fans seeking her autograph she went out of her way to sign herself 'Mrs Frank Sinatra'. MGM had assigned her to pictures with Gable and Robert Taylor. There was also talk of a loan-out to Fox for a big picture with Gregory Peck. Sinatra contemplated that all he had was *Meet Danny Wilson*. It was the *A Star Is Born* equation for real.

Ava was the young star on the rise. Sinatra the one on the skids. It was a situation that led, inevitably to passionate stormy quarrels – that and the fact that Nancy refused to give Frank a divorce.

It was against this background of volatility at home and the continuing uncertainty with Nancy that Sinatra tried to get his act together for *Meet Danny Wilson*. Under the circumstances it was hardly surprising that someone would catch the flak from his edginess and darkness of mood. That someone was his co-star Shelley Winters. She played his songstress girl friend in the picture. They didn't get along. It wasn't long before he was calling her 'a bow-legged bitch' and she was replying in kind with such delicate phrases as 'you stupid Hoboken bastard!' Things continued at roughly the same level throughout shooting.

Like Sinatra, Winters was down to earth. She called a spade a spade. She hadn't enjoyed the easiest route to stardom. Much of it had been a hard grind. She had worked her way up in cheap programmers at Universal. Molls, floozies and girls on the make were her specialities. She had first gained attention as the waitress who is callously murdered by Ronald Colman in his Oscar-winning *A Double Life*. She had just returned from a loan-out to Paramount where she had been working with George Stevens in one of the major productions of the year, *A Place In The Sun*. Her co-stars were Montgomery Clift and Elizabeth Taylor. The film and her performance were already being talked of as possible Oscar contenders. For her, as well as Sinatra, Universal was a bit of a let-down. Hence the aggravation.

Sinatra's songs for the movie were decided by a poll held by 1,500 disc jockeys across America. In May 1951 – designated 'Frank Sinatra Record Month' by Universal – the DJs asked their listeners to send in their favourite Sinatra songs. Universal would then include the top eight songs in the picture. The Tin Pan Alley evergreens chosen by the loyal Sinatra fans included 'That Old Black Magic', 'All Of Me', The Gershwins' 'I've Got a Crush On You' and Irving Berlin's 'How Deep Is The Ocean?'

All except one were solo numbers. There was also a duet, 'A Good Man Is Hard To Find', to be sung with Shelley Winters.

She was unsure as to whether she could handle it. Singing was not exactly her speciality. After working with a director of the stature of George Stevens she had convinced herself that she could handle anything. But singing with Sinatra? That was something else.

Rehearsal time brought panic, a tightening of her vocal chords. She forgot the words. Her timing was wrong. She asked to start again. Sinatra had already demonstrated to everyone on set that he needed to rehearse a number just once and then shoot it. Shelley couldn't. She might have got by if she had been required to sing with a Universal contract star, someone who was her equal. This though was the idol she had swooned over and screamed at as a 20-year-old girl at the Paramount in New York back in 1942.

When she tried again she faltered again. She sensed Sinatra's impatience. More takes. More impatience. A few snarls. A retort from Shelley, 'Who the hell do you think you are?' Before they knew it they were shouting at each other. For Sinatra it was like home from home, shouting with Ava at night, shouting with Shelley during the day. Soon, the phrases incorporating 'bow-legged bitch' and 'Hoboken bastard' were back in play. Director Joseph Pevney, a former actor turned director and a man not accustomed to dealing with such temperament, was left to debate on how best to handle things as the stars stalked off to their respective dressing rooms. 'Just hope for the best' seemed to be the only thing he could come up with.

It was Sinatra who cooled first. He and Shelley tried again. This time he was more understanding, more patient. It may have been that he was genuinely moved by Shelley's obvious plight or it may have been that he realized that the only way they were ever going to get the song done was through co-operation. Whatever the reason, they got through it.

Shelley thought it was the start of a beautiful friendship. Sinatra had refused the studio permission to dub her voice. It was good enough, he said. He also taught her tricks about mouthing back to her voice in close-ups. He seemed to know instinctively when she was secure with a song. The worst is over, thought Shelley. Then came the next row.

It occurred during night shooting at Burbank Airport. The scene required Shelley to tell Sinatra that she didn't, after all, care for him but was in love with his colleague Alex Nicol. All tender, heart-rending stuff. Pevney called for action. Passengers, suddenly realizing that they were in on some movie action stopped to take note. They were surprised at what they saw and even more surprised at what they heard. Instead of a scene from the film they watched the two stars blazing away at each other with words that made even hardened technicians wince.

The language was so lurid that most of the passengers disappeared almost as soon as they had arrived. Once again Pevney did his best to calm things down. He joked that it would be more fun for audiences if he filmed their personal arguments. Neither star found the suggestion funny.

It all ended at three in the morning. Sinatra flew into a terrible rage. Shelley screamed, slugged him in the face and stalked to the edge of the set. Unlike some American-Italians she had known, he didn't hit back. He just slammed into his limousine and roared away. Pevney thankfully called it a night.

The next morning the studio executives were at full stretch trying to placate the two stars. The picture was 99 per cent in the can. All that was needed were a few shots to wrap things up. Would the two stars call a truce? Sinatra was still unhappy. He was in no mood to compromise. The studio sensed that Shelley might be more open to persuasion. They went to work on her, persuading her that he had suffered more than his fair share of troubles, that he was going through a terrible period in his life and that he was still struggling to get back on top as a singer. Shelley climbed down. Shooting was scheduled to restart at 12.30 p.m.

The scene was set in a hospital ward. Sinatra had to say to Shelley and Alex Nicol, 'I'll have a cup of coffee and leave you two lovebirds alone.' They rehearsed it as written. The cameras started rolling. Everything went as planned until they got to the last line. As the camera focused on Sinatra he snorted, 'I'll go and have a cup of Jack Daniels or I'm going to pull that blonde broad's hair out by its black roots.' Shelley was off the set in a flash. It took two days to get her back to the studio. She wouldn't listen to Universal. Only a telephone call from Nancy saying that Sinatra needed the money and if he didn't get any neither would she persuaded Shelley to finish *Meet Danny Wilson*.

It was a good job they did. The scene they were filming was

the last one in the picture. Her agent joked that otherwise Universal would have to release the film with a caption that read, 'Miss Winters and Mr Sinatra do not speak to each other, so this is the end.'

When the scene was set up again Pevney asked for no rehearsals. 'Roll 'em. Action,' he shouted anxiously. This time Sinatra went with the written screenplay, "I'll go have a cup of coffee and leave you two lovebirds alone.' Then he stole the scene by winking into the camera.

For reasons best known to themselves Universal held up the release of *Meet Danny Wilson* until the following spring. Their thinking may have been influenced by Howard Hughes' decision to release at Christmas a piece of nonsense that Sinatra had made three years earlier called *Double Dynamite*. It had been made on a loan out from MGM. Jane Russell and Groucho Marx were Sinatra's co-stars. It was a supposed comedy about a couple of bank-tellers who find themselves $60,000 better off thanks to a grateful bookie. It was a dud. Hughes looked at it, loathed it and shelved it. He should have kept it locked away in the vaults of RKO. With its limp script and mediocre songs – there was a duet with Russell and another with Marx – it did nothing to enhance Sinatra's reputation.

Meet Danny Wilson opened three months later on 26 March, 1952. The critical reaction was low key. Most critics felt that Sinatra was simply playing himself and that there was nothing in the script to extend him. Others, a minority, sensed faint but discernible signs of a dramatic actor beginning to emerge. True, Sinatra knew a character like Danny Wilson inside out, but there was the occasional moment that indicated that Sinatra had learned a thing or two in his years in front of a movie camera. The critic of *Newsweek* said, 'Sinatra is responsible for most of the picture's interest, a convincing portrayal of a nasty little success boy and, as usual, a finely relaxed singer of some excellent popular songs.' Kay Proctor in the *Los Angeles Examiner* remarked 'Sinatra the actor? For the first time on the screen he seems completely at ease and sure of himself and of what he is doing.'

Sinatra did his best to give the picture something of a send-off by appearing for a two-week engagement at the Paramount when it opened in March 1952. The idea misfired.

The balcony in the theatre held 750 seats. At most performances only a handful of those seats were filled. It was difficult to imagine that just a decade earlier those same seats had been packed with screaming riotous kids.

But if March 1952 went down as an unsuccessful month in the Sinatra cannon, at least 1951 ended happily. Nancy at last agreed to a divorce. A week later, on 7 November, Frank and Ava were married. The marriage took place at a friend's house in West Germantown, Pennsylvania. No newsmen were allowed at the ceremony. Photographs were released the next day. The couple honeymooned in Miami and Cuba. For a few days it was bliss. No movies, no press, no publicity. It didn't last. The press got wind of where they were and descended *en masse*. Frank and Ava departed their hotel so quickly Ava didn't have time to pack her clothes. She left her entire wardrobe behind.

6 From Here to Eternity

'I know Maggio. I *really* know him. I grew
up with people like him as a kid in
Hoboken.'

Frank Sinatra

It was a joke! At least Columbia boss Harry Cohn thought it
was. Frank Sinatra was after one of the key roles in Cohn's film
version of *From Here to Eternity*, James Jones's sprawling
bestseller of military life in a Honolulu barracks just prior to
Pearl Harbor. The part Sinatra was seeking was that of Private
Maggio, a rebellious little Italian-American with a grudge
against the army, who grins and boozes his way through life
before dying at the hands of a brutal stockade sergeant. It was
one of the five key roles in the movie.

Cohn scoffed at the idea. 'Maggio's an acting part,' he said.
'Sinatra's a singer. Tell him we don't have any songs in *From
Here To Eternity*.' Sinatra was not deterred. 'I *know* Maggio,' he
said in newspaper interviews. 'I *really* know him. I grew up with
people like him as a kid in Hoboken. I was beaten up by guys
like him. I might have been Maggio. I know exactly the way he
thinks and acts.'

Harry Cohn remained unimpressed by Sinatra's public
utterances. For him Sinatra was no actor. He was already a
has-been in movies. He had too many of those hanging around
the Columbia lot. He didn't want anymore.

Sinatra though, hung in. He said again, 'I *am* Maggio.' He
said it again to the press and he said it to his agent who badgered
Columbia twice, three times, sometimes four times a day. When

that approach drew a blank Sinatra tried a different tack. He sent cables to Cohn, to the film's producer Buddy Adler and to director Fred Zinnemann. He signed each one of them 'Maggio'. Again, no response.

The only thing working in his favour was that Cohn and Zinnemann had decided to leave the casting of Maggio to last which at least allowed Sinatra time to think up a few other ploys. As he figured out new ways to ingratiate himself with Harry Cohn, the Columbia boss and his director concerned themselves with the other four leads. They named Montgomery Clift as the doomed bugler Private Prewitt, Burt Lancaster as the tough Sergeant Warden and Donna Reed as the call-girl Lorene. The role of Karen Holmes, the company commander's sleep-around wife, gave them trouble. Cohn argued for Joan Crawford. Zinnemann suggested that casting against type might be a better idea. He threw a hand grenade into the works. How about Deborah Kerr? Cohn gasped. Deborah Kerr was a typical English rose. Her studio, MGM, had cast her primarily in historical epics and swashbucklers in which she was always the demure heroine. No one would believe that she'd been round the block and back. Besides there was a sexy beach scene with Burt Lancaster. Cohn took an aspirin. *Deborah Kerr!*

Zinnemann wouldn't give up. 'Harry, people will be fascinated. If you cast Joan Crawford people will say, "OK, she's cast as a tramp, so what else is new?" But with Deborah ... Think of the publicity.' Cohn remained unconvinced. Crawford was approached. She didn't like the idea of being billed behind Burt Lancaster and Montgomery Clift and she certainly didn't like her wardrobe. Something would have to be done about that. Suddenly, Zinnemann's suggestion of Deborah Kerr seemed more attractive. Cohn gave in. He wanted the picture to be trouble free. It would be expensive – $2 million. He wanted it brought in quickly. Kerr was signed.

That left Maggio. Sinatra was still hopeful. If Deborah Kerr could get to grips with promiscuity why couldn't he have a shot at a little Italian-American private?

It was a question brought up by Ava when she attended a dinner party at Harry Cohn's house just prior to her leaving for Africa for John Ford's *Mogambo*. She had been invited to see if she could be tempted into appearing in a movie called *Joseph*

49

And His Brethren. Cohn had been saddled with a lot of second unit footage shot in Egypt. He needed a script and a star to go with it. Perhaps Ava might be interested?

Ava was not in the least interested but she cannily kept her options open. She hinted that she might just be available if her MGM schedule allowed. She added that she would certainly think it over, mentioning in the same breath that her husband still had an all-consuming interest in Maggio. It hadn't been cast yet, had it? she asked coyly. Harry Cohn was at the far end of the table. He just growled.

Later that evening Ava confided to Cohn's wife Joan that Frank was broke and also in debt. There were no movie offers on the horizon. He owed thousands in back taxes. He was desperate. Ava and Joan had been friends for years. Joan assured her that she would use her wiles on Harry.

A few days later Sinatra was invited to lunch by Harry Cohn. The Columbia boss was still hostile. In his view Sinatra was bad news both on and off the screen. He believed he warranted nothing better than B musicals, the kind he was currently assigning to other singers trying to break into the business – Frankie Laine and Billy Daniels, pictures like *Rainbow Round My Shoulder* and *Cruisin' Down The River*.

'You must be out of your fucking mind wanting to do this,' he said over lunch. 'I had you pegged as a singer in a sailor suit.'

Sinatra knew the lunch would be an ordeal. Cohn would enjoy making him squirm.

'Harry I can do this, I know I can … just give me a chance. I know more about movies than just musicals. My last one, *Meet Danny Wilson* …'

'A dog, it died.'

'Yeah, but …'

Cohn was impatient. He brushed the film aside. He said curtly, 'Look, I'll come clean with you. Zinnemann wants Eli Wallach for the role so we're testing him. Harvey Lembeck's also interested so we're giving him a test as well. Why should we test you? Just give me one good reason.'

Wallach's test was bad news for Sinatra. Wallach was a fine actor. He'd made his name on the Broadway stage. *Eternity* would be his movie début. The very fact that he was being considered spelt danger. Sinatra played the only card he had.

'I'll give you a reason,' he said to Cohn across the luncheon table. 'I'll do it for a thousand a week.'

The offer stopped Cohn dead in his tracks. It was the one answer he hadn't expected. He laid down his fork and stared hard at Sinatra. Even the lowly Universal had paid the singer $25,000 for *Meet Danny Wilson*. At Metro in the late forties Sinatra had been getting $150,000 a picture. The most he would get from an eight-week shoot on *From Here To Eternity* was $8,000. Cohn had paid ten times that just to buy the rights.

'You want the part that bad?' he said softly. He shook his head. 'I'll think about it Frank. Leave it with me.' The two men remained in pensive mood for the rest of the lunch. Few stars had sold themselves so cheap before, even to Harry Cohn.

It might have been Sinatra's cut price offer or it might have been the memory of Al Jolson that caused Cohn to soften his attitude. In the mid forties Jolson had also been a washed up performer. Until Harry Cohn had put him back on the map in *The Jolson Story*. Cohn had made the film when no other studio would touch it. It started a whole new career for Jolson. It had been one of the biggest comebacks in movie history. Perhaps history would repeat itself if Sinatra did *Eternity*. Either way, Cohn figured he had nothing to lose – a big name for just $8,000!

Sinatra was in Africa with Ava when the cable arrived telling him he would be screen tested for Maggio. He was cock-a-hoop. Ava's co-star Clark Gable warned him to keep his feet on the ground. He'd been in movies for nearly twenty-five years and seen it all. 'Talent is the least important thing in this business Frank,' he said. 'Humility is the thing you really need. Remember that.'

The plane journey from Africa to Los Angeles was 27,000 miles. It is doubtful whether any actor before or since had travelled such a distance for a fifteen-minute screen test. Sinatra, or, as was more likely, Ava, paid the fare.

Sinatra was required to perform two scenes for his test. The first was when he is slightly inebriated and joking with some friends at a bar. To demonstrate a point he uses a couple of olives as dice and rolls them across the top of a bar. The second scene was when he is found drunk outside the Royal Hawaiian Hotel. He gave both scenes all he had. Nerves nearly got the better of him but his acting was sharp and convincing. Zinnemann was impressed. So was producer Buddy Adler.

Hollywood wisdom has it that Harry Cohn was so bowled over by Sinatra's test that he signed him then and there. Sinatra, however, was left dangling, and for good reason. Eli Wallach had given by far the best test of the three actors and been offered the part. Sinatra had come in a good second; Harvey Lembeck, a comedian who was all wrong for the role, finished a distant third. Sinatra, still believing the role was wide open and unaware that it had been offered to Wallach, returned to Africa and waited.

The problem with Wallach was that he had previously made a commitment to director Elia Kazan to appear in a new Tennessee Williams play called *Camino Real*. If Kazan got backing Wallach would do the play. If not he would play Maggio. The situation was resolved when Kazan cabled that the play was on. Wallach duly headed for New York. Another version of events has it that Wallach's agent was greedy regarding terms and asked twice as much as Cohn was willing to pay. Whatever the reason, Wallach chose Broadway and delayed his screen career by some five years.

Yet even with Wallach out of the running Cohn still dithered. Incredibly, he worried that with Sinatra's name above the title, audiences might think he was turning James Jones's book into a musical. His wife Joan told him he was crazy and that the picture was getting to him.

In the end, it was Joan who made up his mind for him. She watched all the tests and said that, in her mind, there was no doubt. Even if Wallach had accepted the role he was too muscular. Maggio needed to be skinny. The character required sympathy from the audience. Sinatra was skinny. He was short. He had tested well. Why look any further. Sinatra was signed.

Eternity's screenwriter Daniel Taradash observed, 'Frank got the part by default. He was so thin and woeful. So pitiful.' He added with a wry smile that his getting the role had nothing to do with a horse's head, an incident depicted in *The Godfather* as being instrumental in getting a singer a key film role because of his links with organized crime.

Once filming got under way Zinnemann shot fast. Harry Cohn had decreed that *From Here To Eternity* should cost not a cent more than the $2 million allowed. Another prerequisite was that 120 minutes should be the maximum running time. The human bladder, Cohn believed could take no more than a two-hour movie. Cohn also wanted the film brought in on schedule in just eight weeks – not a day longer. Despite an expensive cast – Montgomery Clift alone cost 150,000 dollars – and a lengthy location shoot in Hawaii, producer Adler kept within the targets.

The entire company was transported by charter plane to Hawaii, arriving at 5 a.m. By mid morning exterior shooting had begun at Schofield Army Barracks. Cohn denied Zinnemann's request that the company be given a day for sightseeing in the islands. Rushes were viewed and edited on the spot. As soon as the location scenes were in the can, the cast and crew were flown back to complete the picture in Hollywood.

For most of the time filming went smoothly. Harry Cohn, anxious to keep a high profile, ensconced himself at the Royal Hawaiian Hotel where he kept the company of the top military brass. 'Harry's arse-lickin' vacation' as some crew members referred to it.

In Cohn's defence he didn't really have much option. He was making a movie of a book they had said couldn't be filmed. Sex, sadism and four-letter words were its key ingredients. He was showing the army in an unfavourable light and focusing on corruption, crooked officers and brutality among enlisted men. He knew he had to tread carefully. The army had requested minor changes but none that would affect the picture in any major way. As shooting in Honolulu neared its close he thought he'd made it to the wire. Then came trouble. Cohn received news that a scene involving Sinatra and Clift had been changed without any prior notification.

The scene was one of those Sinatra had tested for, when he is found on a bench, drunk and half-dressed, 'waiting for a movie-star to come along'. Clift raises him to a sitting position with Sinatra all the time complaining bitterly about the army and how he has been harassed beyond endurance by the service. When he sees two military policemen heading in his direction he charges at them with his shoe, berating them wildly. One of the cops grabs him round the waist, the other tries to grab his feet. 'Is that the best you can do?' splutters Sinatra, still swinging.

Thump! A punch from one of the MPs hits the mark and Sinatra goes limp.

Most of the scene is played with Sinatra seated. Only in the last few seconds does he rise and attack the MPs. Sinatra, however, had suggested that the scene might be more effective if he mouthed his tirade against the army whilst standing. Zinnemann could see no objections. Sinatra's interpretation might improve the scene. He went along with the idea.

The scene was due to be shot in the early evening. Rehearsals had gone well and Zinnemann was just in the act of calling 'action' when Cohn, who up until that point, had carefully avoided interfering with filming, arrived on the set. He was clad in a white dinner jacket and smoking a cigar. His face was red. He was not pleased. He was also not alone. General O'Daniel, the man in charge of the entire Pacific Air Force, was by his side. The garrison's top echelon of officers made up the descending force. Not one of them looked happy.

'What the hell is going on here?' roared Cohn at the top of his voice. He glared at Zinnemann. 'You're changing this scene. I want this scene played as scripted.' He turned to Sinatra. 'How dare you tell a director what to do. You shoot the picture the way I tell you or I'm going to shut it down!'

Zinnemann had seen Cohn's rages before. Sometimes they were an act, designed to frighten people. Sometimes they were for real. This one was genuine, inspired he felt by military voices that in no way would stand for any changes.

The set fell quiet. Cohn fumed. Sinatra glared back. Zinnemann shifted uncomfortably. Something or someone had to give. They were on army territory. Zinnemann felt that Cohn was bluffing but he decided not to call it. They were only minor changes anyway. He pulled back. 'OK,' he said. 'We'll go with the script'. Sinatra instantly became moody, sullen and unhappy. He had no option but to play the scene as instructed. He didn't speak to Zinnemann for weeks. 'I couldn't blame him for being upset,' said Zinnemann later, 'but I wonder whether he knew what was at stake'.

Zinnemann's only other problem on the picture was when he had to reduce one of his favourite scenes, the one in which Maggio dies in Clift's arms and is carried carefully to a truck where Clift says tenderly, 'Mind his head, don't bump.' It was only a few seconds of screen time but it never made it into the final movie. Cohn was a terror for saving time. Two hours remained the maximum running time. The scene ends with Burt Lancaster kneeling over Sinatra and saying simply, 'He's dead.' The screen then fades to black.

Cohn smelt Oscars with *From Here To Eternity*. He had the most publicized film of the year on his hands. He also had that very rare commodity, a Hollywood picture that actually lived up to all the hype. He booked it into the Capitol Theatre in New York on 5 August 1953. It was unheard of to open a major film in the middle of the summer holiday season but Cohn had no doubts. He even restricted all advertising for the film to a full page advertisement in the *New York Times*. He personally signed the announcement, urging people to see the film. In 1953 there was no air conditioning in cinemas. All movie-houses were sweat boxes. It mattered not at all. From the moment the film opened queues spread their way around the block. An extra show was hastily arranged for a one o'clock morning show. The only time the theatre was closed was when the janitor arrived to clean up.

From Here To Eternity didn't really need good reviews but it got them anyway. Critics praised Zinnemann's handling and Taradash's script, many going as far as to maintain that together they had actually succeeded in improving on Jones's original novel. So beautifully realized was the picture that it appeared seamless, weaving its way effortlessly from one scene to the next, fully developing each character and brilliantly sustaining its atmosphere of time and place. Visually striking without once seeming flashy, it emerged as a cohesive and gripping drama, spiced with action, outhouse vulgarity and easy ladies.

The famous beach scene between Lancaster and Kerr inevitably attracted the greatest comment but most believed, rightly, that the film belonged to Monty Clift and Sinatra. Sinatra didn't need anyone to tell him that he'd made it as Maggio. He'd felt it in his bones everytime Zinnemann had called 'Action' on the set. And he'd been tutored in the art of dramatic acting by the man who, more than any other knew all the subtleties and nuances of performing before the cameras, Monty Clift.

Sinatra was on screen less than any of the other principal

performers but he made every minute count. In his death scene he was superb, broken, bloody, hardly able to speak. *Variety* said, 'Frank Sinatra scores a decided hit as Angelo Maggio ... while some may be amazed at this expression of the Sinatra talent versatility, it will come as no surprise to those who remember the few times he has had a chance to be something other than a crooner in films.' The *Los Angeles Examiner* added, 'He is simply superb, comical, pitiful, childishly brave, pathetically defiant.' *Time* was equally enthusiastic, 'Frank Sinatra does Private Maggio like nothing he has ever done before. His face wears the calm of a man who is completely sure of what he is doing as he plays straight from Little Italy.'

The *Newsweek* critic wrote, 'Sinatra can act when the mood is on him and when the writing is good.'

It was that last phrase that really hit the mark. *When the writing is good!* Previously Sinatra had not had a worthwhile script to get his teeth into. His scriptwriters had been mostly hacks, Hollywood journeymen employed on routine assignments. His MGM musicals didn't really need scripts, just songs. Now he had shown what he could do not only with a fine script but under the direction of one of Hollywood's finest craftsmen. Zinnemann, carefully and subtly kept the Sinatra mannerisms in check, allowing the Sinatra persona to emerge only occasionally. Zinnemann summed up Sinatra as being 'wonderful to work with 90 per cent of the time – the other 10 per cent he was objectionable and loud'.

A member of the production crew added, 'When he first walked on that set he was like a school kid playing hookey with the adults. Then he kind of filled out and his head went back and he started looking you straight in the eye again. And when he walked off at the end of the picture he walked out like he was king once more.

When he arrived in New York to promote the film with the other stars he could see the crowds winding their way round the Capitol Theatre. The crowds reminded him of those at the Paramount Theatre a decade before. The Capitol crowds weren't for him alone this time. But they were partly for him. He smiled with satisfaction. He had got his triumph. He was back.

7 Pink Tights

'There's a guy who's wandering around
the lot who you're paying $5,000 a week
not to make a picture.'

Sammy Cahn

Zanuck moved fast once *From Here To Eternity* began breaking box-office records. His offer to Sinatra was a CinemaScope musical at Fox called *Pink Tights*. Sinatra's co-star would be Marilyn Monroe. She was fresh from her triumphs in *Niagara, Gentlemen Prefer Blondes* and *How To Marry A Millionaire*. Sinatra's fee would be $5,000 a week. He said 'yes'. Monroe's fee would be $1,500 a week. She said 'no'.

She also said a lot of other things besides. She didn't like the story – a mission girl in the Bowery finds herself involved in show business – she didn't like the script, it was trite, and she didn't like the costumes. In fact, she didn't like anything about the movie which she considered to be just another piece of junk off the CinemaScope assembly line. She'd just finished shooting the yet unreleased western *River Of No Return* which she'd already described as 'a Z movie in which the story came second to the scenery and Cinemascope'. She felt the same way about *Pink Tights*. The message to Zanuck was clear. He could take his movie and shove it!

'Pique-temperament-ego-bluster,' smiled the benign German-born director Henry Koster who had been assigned to turn *Pink Tights* into a masterpiece. 'Marilyn's a contract star. She knows what she can and can't do. She'll come round.'

Koster's confidence turned out to be misplaced. Marilyn

didn't come round. The Marilyn he had known a year before when he'd directed her in a walk-on part in the omnibus movie *O'Henry's Full House* had been very different from the all-important star who now ruled the Fox lot. Any hopes that she might settle her quarrel with Zanuck and make an appearance as shooting got under way were quickly dashed. There was no sign of her on day one, nor day two or three. A week went by and still no Marilyn. After two weeks news began to filter through that Zanuck had put her on suspension and that the picture was on hold. A new star was being considered.

It was a false rumour. No new star appeared. Sinatra went back to making business deals on the telephone, co-stars Dan Dailey, Van Johnson and Mitzi Gaynor chewed over the state of the movie business, and choreographer Bob Alton did his best to instil some enthusiasm among those involved in the dance routines. The general view of the technicians, who tinkered daily with the CinemaScope equipment, was that *Pink Tights* would never be made and that everyone would be paid off. Most were philosophical. What the hell, it had happened before. It would happen again.

Yet out of all this mess came a stroke of luck, at least for Sinatra and songwriters Sammy Cahn and Jule Styne. Things looked up when a top Fox producer, Sol Siegel, paid a hurried visit to the set. He looked distinctly harassed. Just the sight of someone who looked as though he had actually been working was comforting to the *Pink Tights* crew. Siegel sought out Sammy Cahn who was wistfully playing one of his songs on the piano.

'Sammy, you busy?' The question brought ironic laughter from all those within earshot. 'OK, OK,' said Siegel wearily. 'I know all the problems but right now I've got troubles of my own. I need a song and I need it in a hurry.'

'You want a song, I've got ten of 'em,' said Cahn with a wry smile. 'They've all been written for this picture – you know, the one they're never going to make. Be my guest. Take your pick.'

Siegel shook his head. 'That's not it. I need a title song Sammy, something for a picture that's already been shot, something to go behind the credits.'

Cahn shrugged. He had nothing to lose. 'OK, fine, let's see it.'

'Can't be done. The damn thing's all over the lot being dubbed and scored and re-edited. Its a mess.'

'So what's your problem?'

Siegel sighed, 'Politics Sammy, politics. Darryl and the New York Office are at loggerheads. New York want to call the thing *We Believe In Love*. Darryl hates the title, loathes it, believes it will kill the film stone dead. He wants it called *Three Coins In The Fountain*. He reckons that the only way he can persuade them is if we come up with a catchy title song. Then he believes he can swing it.' Siegel paused. 'But we do need it like yesterday.'

'Well, you can at least tell me what the movie's about,' said Cahn.

'It's about three girls who go to Rome. They make a wish by throwing three coins in the Trevi Fountain. Their wishes come true when each of them meets and falls in love with a man.'

'That's it?'

'Yeah, that's it.'

'OK.' And with that Cahn and composer Jule Styne got to work on a slow romantic ballad that took them just two hours to write in one afternoon on the Fox lot. The opening lines were conjured up by Cahn in the first few minutes, 'Three coins in the fountain, each one seeking happiness, thrown by three hopeful lovers, which one will the fountain bless?'

'Love it,' said a relieved Siegel. 'We'll demonstrate it to Darryl.'

'Where?' asked Cahn.

'In his office,' replied Siegel.

Cahn needed no second bidding. He liked nothing better than an audience especially if that audience was the head of one of Hollywood's major studios. 'Mr Zanuck,' he said. 'I have a song for your new movie. I hope you like it.' And so saying he launched into the first few bars of 'Three Coins In The Fountain'.

Zanuck was still fuming over losing *Pink Tights* from his schedules. He was determined not to lose another one of his key films. He listened without a word, smiling as Cahn, by no means the greatest singer in the world, went into overdrive with the closing lyrics, 'Make it mine, make it mine, make it mine!'

Like Siegel, Zanuck had no doubts. 'Great ... Sol get me a demonstration disc. We'll send it to New York.'

'Who would you suggest?' asked Siegel.

'Get Sammy to do it', smiled Zanuck. 'If he can convince me I guess he can convince them.' Cahn, a small, balding, bespectacled man with a moustache, was stunned. He said, 'I have a better suggestion Mr Zanuck.'

'What's that?'

'Well, there's a guy who's wandering around the lot who you're paying $5,000 a week not to make a picture – Sinatra.'

'Will he do it?'

'He'll do it.'

Cahn sounded confident but he knew he had some conniving to do. Sinatra had a temper. If he was not in the mood and if he was approached in the wrong way he would be more than likely to tell you to go f... yourself. Cahn decided on a plan of campaign.

First, he and Styne made an arrangement of the song and sent it across to the studio's composer/arranger Lionel Newman who was then working with the studio orchestra on the score of an upcoming CinemaScope epic about ancient Rome. 'Frank doesn't know about this,' he confided to Newman, 'but play along with it if you can. Zanuck needs this song – and fast.' Next came the 'con'.

'Hi Frank,' he said cheerily, as he strolled onto the *Pink Tights* set.

'What's new?' asked Sinatra glumly.

'Well at least something good's come out of this mess. Zanuck wants a demo record for that movie of his, you know the one that was shot in Rome, *Three Coins In The Fountain*.'

'Yeah, who's doing it?'

'Me.'

Sinatra chuckled, '*You* ... you got a voice like a vain duck with a hangover. What's wrong with me?'

'Nothing Frank, nothing ... you want to do it. No problem. It's fine by me.'

Sinatra shrugged, 'Why not, there isn't much else going on around here.'

The sting was made. Sinatra went over the song with Sammy and acquainted himself with the lyrics. It didn't take long. It was an easy song. 'OK, let's do it,' he said. Together they strolled across to the recording studio. Sinatra pushed through the doors ahead of Sammy. The moment of truth. 'What the hell ... ' began Sinatra.

Ahead of him sat the sixty musicians of the Fox studio

orchestra. On the podium, his baton raised in a kind of mock 'What the hell are we waiting for?' gesture, was conductor Lionel Newman.

Sinatra gave Cahn a jaundiced look and said, 'I thought this was going to be a simple demo with you and Jule at the piano.'

'Yeah Frank, but these guys just happened to be here and ... ' Another jaundiced look. This time there was humour too.

'They just happen to be here and they just happen to have an orchestration in my key?'

'Yeah Frank, they just happen to have an orchestration in your key.'

Sinatra raised his eyes. Cahn got in quick, 'But don't worry Frank. If you'd rather do it with Jule at the piano I can have these guys take five.'

'Take *five*. It'll take them half an hour to get out of here. Let's hear the orchestration.'

Ten minutes later he made the record. There were no other recordings. The demonstration disc was the one used on the soundtrack of the movie. When the film was released in 1954 Sinatra's record remained in the charts for three months. Twelve months later Sammy Cahn and Jule Styne received the ultimate accolade – the Oscar for the best song of the year.

In the end *Pink Tights* was never made. The technicians had been right in their prophecies. There was talk of making it at a later date with Sinatra and Bob Hope in a key role. Then it slid down a notch or two when it was resurrected as a possible vehicle for Johnny Ray and Sheree North. After that it vanished from the schedules. It was never heard of again.

At least Sinatra and Cahn and Styne had no regrets. They had come out ahead. So too, for that matter, had Marilyn Monroe. She married baseball legend Joe DiMaggio and went on honeymoon to Japan. She followed that with a ten-day tour entertaining the troops at American military bases in South Korea. She felt that that was a somewhat better idea than appearing in the movie. She almost certainly made the right decision.

8 The End of the Affair

> I like Frank now but at the time I hated
> the little bastard because he was making
> Ava unhappy. Now I understand him. He
> was so beaten and insecure.'
>
> Casey Robinson

The last rites were announced by MGM's publicity director Howard Strickling. His statement was simple and to the point, 'Ava Gardner and Frank Sinatra stated today that, having reluctantly exhausted every effort to reconcile their differences, they could find no mutual basis on which to continue their marriage. Both expressed deep regret and great respect for each other. Their separation is final and Miss Gardner will seek a divorce.'

No one was surprised. The marriage had lasted for just under two years. Columnist Earl Wilson said, 'Their marriage was a two-year soap opera with screaming fights heard around the world.'

Ava's summing up of the separation was typically down to earth, 'I guess we were trapped. We couldn't live with each other and we couldn't live without each other. We simply didn't know which way to go.'

A devastated Sinatra preferred to keep his own counsel.

For those outside as well as inside Hollywood the main reason for the break-up was plain to see. During their two years together as man and wife, Ava was constantly 'up' and Sinatra permanently 'down'. Some would say 'out'. Ava, at the height of her beauty and with her hour-glass figure of 36-20-36, was described by magazines as 'The world's most beautiful animal!' MGM put it somewhat differently. They preferred the publicity line, 'She's sultry enough to melt the North Pole.' Those in the real world, The United Elevator Operators of America, voted her the girl they would most like to be stuck with at the top of the Empire State Building.

No one, it seemed, wanted to be stuck with Sinatra in or at the top of anything. He was no longer the world's best crooner. Not anymore. Until *From Here To Eternity* he would still be referred to as 'Mr Ava Gardner'.

One of the earliest problems in their marriage occurred when Metro loaned Ava to Fox for a role in their adaptation of Ernest Hemingway's celebrated short story, *The Snows of Kilimanjaro*. The film was a large-scale production and the studio's most ambitious undertaking of 1952. Studio boss Darryl F. Zanuck was at the helm as producer and the co-stars were Gregory Peck and Susan Hayward. It was a big step up for Ava.

The problem was that it clashed with an equally big moment for Sinatra. He had been playing club dates that were way beneath him. Out of the blue came the offer of an important singing engagement in New York. It was a break but he needed reassurance. He wanted Ava with him. He requested she be there.

For Ava, it meant either a huge, fractious row with Frank or dropping out of the movie altogether. She discussed the problem with director Henry King and writer Casey Robinson. They told her that they couldn't afford to lose her. After consulting with Zanuck they rearranged the shooting schedule. All of Ava's scenes would be shot in the first ten days. That way she could make the picture *and* be with Frank.

All went well until the tenth day when Fox informed Ava that they would need her for an extra day's shooting. They were filming a Spanish Civil War scene that involved hundreds of extras. It was a complicated set-up. They couldn't do it without her. 'Frank gave me holy hell about it,' said Ava. 'I knew he would. I tried to explain that I couldn't get out of it and that I had no option but it wasn't any good. By God, did he let me know about that!'

Casey Robinson remembered, 'He kept calling her on set and making her life pretty damn miserable. I like Frank now but at the time I hated the little bastard because he was making Ava unhappy. Now I understand him. He was so beaten and insecure.'

The Snows Of Kilimanjaro offered Ava one of her most rewarding roles, that of Cynthia Green, a lady who is very much her own woman and who lives with struggling writer Gregory Peck in the Paris of the twenties. In one of the film's key sequences, when their relationship is beginning to fall apart, she finds herself getting slowly drunk at a dinner table while making eyes at a Spanish flamenco dancer. She turns away, looks at Peck and utters the mocking line, 'We're so hopelessly in love, why can't we make it work?' The stoney-faced look on Peck's face indicates that he has no answer.

In real life, Sinatra had no answer either. He was similarly perplexed. His jealousy of Ava and hers of him, continued unabated as did the fiery rows and shouting matches. On one occasion he finished up throwing both Ava and Lana Turner, plus a few other things besides, out of his home in Palm Springs because they were mocking him behind his back. It was three in the morning. The police were called. The police chief was a friend of Frank's and calmed things down. Sinatra though, stalked off to Jimmy Van Heusen's house. He was back with Ava a few days later but not before more harsh words had been exchanged.

Ava consoled herself with the fact that at least it hadn't been as bad as an episode that had occurred in the days before their marriage, one that had revolved around her ex-husband, band-leader Artie Shaw. Frank was singing at the Copacabana at the time. Ava was there, every night, in the audience. Always she would be seated in the same place.

One night she was missing. She had decided to skip a performance to catch up with some gossip with Shaw who had just arrived in town with his new girlfriend. Shaw had an apartment in New York. Ava dropped in to talk about old times and how she was getting on with Frank. Unwisely, she left a note telling Frank where she was.

Later, when he returned to the Hampshire House Hotel and read the note Sinatra jumped to the wrong conclusion. He rang Ava's adjoining suite in the hotel. He was convinced that Ava and Artie had slept together. 'I can't stand it any longer, I'm

The shy and nervous boy next-door! Sinatra in his first starring role in *Higher And Higher* and sharing things here with *(left to right)* Mary Wickes, Jack Haley and Michèle Morgan

Sinatra and Gene Kelly together for the first time and about to embark on shore leave in Los Angeles in the MGM musical *Anchors Aweigh*

Fun and games with Jimmy Durante in the musical comedy *It Happened In Brooklyn*. Sinatra and Durante shared the number 'The song's gotta come from the heart'

New York, New York...sailors Sinatra, Jules Munshin and Gene Kelly
on the loose in The Big Apple in the classic MGM musical *On The Town*

Mixing it on the way to the top! Night-club singer Sinatra being
restrained by partner Alex Nicol in *Meet Danny Wilson*

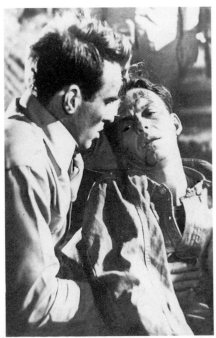

The two faces of Sinatra in *From Here To Eternity*. *Above:* enjoying the pleasures of a twenty-four hour pass in Honolulu. *Left:* close to death in the arms of Montgomery Clift after escaping from the stockade

Saloon singer meets small-town gal! Sinatra and Doris Day in *Young At Heart*

As would-be-presidential assassin John Baron in the thriller, *Suddenly*

'Who Wants To Be A Millionaire?'. One of Sinatra's best songs of the fifties, sung in *High Society* with Celeste Holm

Together at last! Sinatra and Crosby with Cole Porter's 'Well, Did You Evah?' in *High Society*

The moment of defeat! Sinatra succumbs to his addiction in Otto Preminger's powerful *The Man With The Golden Arm*

As one of Mike Todd's forty guest stars in *Around The World In Eighty Days*. Also offering cameos in this scene are Red Skelton and George Raft

going to kill myself now,' was all Ava heard as she picked up the receiver – that and two loud bangs. She rushed into his suite. Sinatra was lying on the bed, pale and shaking. He had fired a revolver into the mattress. He looked up at her in an exhausted fashion and said simply, 'Oh, hello!'. It took more than an hour to convince the desk clerk and a couple of police officers that no gun had been fired. Ava said later that she was sure no one believed them but as they found no gun (carefully buried beneath her pillow) things went no further.

The biggest setback for Sinatra was with his music. Mitch Miller's dire prophecies about his style going permanently out of fashion seemed to be coming true with a vengeance. In December 1952, Columbia refused to renew his recording contract. There were no other takers. The biggest blow of all came when MCA announced that they would no longer represent him. They claimed that he owed them $40,000 in back commission. 'They'll never let me go,' said Sinatra to the trade papers. 'Not someone who last year earned $700,000.'

Let him go they did, however. Sinatra was suddenly a man without a recording company, an agency or a movie studio. All he had to fall back on were his club dates. They did, at least, allow him to keep with the standards and 'the good stuff': 'London By Night', 'April In Paris', the poignant 'Why Try To Change Me Now?' and 'I'm A Fool To Love You' which he wrote as a token of his seemingly hopeless love for Ava. But even his club dates brought him face to face with bleak reality. When he played Chez Paree in Chicago he pulled in just 150 patrons. The club's capacity was 1,200.

It was only after the completion of *From Here To Eternity* that Sinatra at last began to believe that he had broken 'the jinx'. In the summer of 1953 he made one last attempt to patch things up with Ava. He had seen a preview of *Eternity* and was buoyant. His musical luck had also changed. He had signed with Capitol Records and was working with arranger/conductor Nelson Riddle. A tour of Europe would round things off nicely. He could join Ava for a second honeymoon in England where she was filming a piece of historical nonsense called *Knights Of The Round Table*. There had been second honeymoons before, plenty of them. This one would turn out no better than the rest.

Things came to a head when Ava took a few days off from

filming to join Frank in Europe. It soon became obvious that the public were more interested in seeing Ava than they were in listening to Frank. In Naples, when he was halfway through a song, noisy patrons shouted, 'Ava, Ava, Ava!' The spotlight turned from the stage and picked out Ava in the audience. She had no alternative but to acknowledge the applause. The orchestra stopped playing. Sinatra walked from the stage. He returned later but it was obvious that he had felt the humiliation. As the tour progressed he played to half-empty houses in Rome, Copenhagen and Malmo in Sweden.

None of which helped his mood when he and Ava returned to London. There were skirmishes at the airport and angry incidents with journalists. In an attempt to keep away from the constant glare of publicity they rented an apartment rather than stay at a hotel. Nothing though would discourage the press. They hung on, waiting for the next crisis.

At the apartment, instead of the hoped for reconciliation, there was bickering. There were fights and fights and yet more fights. One was so loud it brought complaints from the neighbours. Another, equally as loud, had Sinatra storming out of the apartment only to find himself locked out on his return and having to hammer on the door for Ava to let him in.

Later, when a journalist suggested that if they had had children it might have saved their relationship, Ava shook her head vehemently. She had undergone two abortions with Frank. The first when she was making *Mogambo* in Africa and had flown to London for the operation, the second six months later at a small clinic in Wimbledon. No kids was her rule. It was more her idea than his. She wasn't exactly enamoured of her career as a movie-star but it did allow her a certain freedom and she wasn't going to give it all up to become domesticated. 'We didn't exactly have the right kind of life style to have kids,' she said later. 'Frank would arrive home at about 4 a.m. after a singing engagement at a nightclub or a concert and I would have to leave the house at 6.30 a.m. or earlier to get to the studio on time. Not really much of a home life there. Besides, I guess we were both too selfish to have kids.'

When Sinatra was due to return to the States to play an engagement in New Jersey he flew back alone. Ava, having finished her epic, arrived in New York a few days later. Frank was not at the airport to meet her. She moved into the Hampshire House Hotel. He stayed at the Waldorf Towers. Each waited for the other to call. Neither did. When Frank opened at Bill Miller's Riviera in Englewood, Ava went to the première of a Broadway show.

When the end finally came on 29 October 1953 with Strickling's terse announcement they were both worn out, both close to a nervous breakdown. They had nothing left to fight each other with. Said Ava, 'Our love was so battered and bruised we simply couldn't take it any more.' Sinatra said sadly, 'If Ava says it's over then I guess it's over ... If it took seventy-five years to get a divorce there would be no other woman.'

There were other women of course, plenty of them in the years that followed but for Sinatra there was never another Ava. It took four years from the time of the official announcement of separation for the divorce to become final. During those four years they saw each other many times. For all the fighting and bickering they remained friends and remained so until Ava's sudden death in 1990. He would call. She would call. They never seemed to be far from each other's thoughts. Sometimes he would suggest that they try again. She needed no second bidding. She would drop everything, sometimes even a part in a picture, and join him wherever he happened to be at the time – New York, London, Rome, Madrid. 'It would be heaven', said Ava. 'But it wouldn't last for more than 24 hours. And I'd go running off again, literally running. We could never quite understand why it hadn't and couldn't work out.'

9 Oscar Night

'If I start thanking everybody I'll do a
one-reeler.'

Frank Sinatra

Sinatra kept remembering the words of Monty Clift. 'This role
could win you an Oscar, Frank,' he'd said almost a year before
when they had watched the rushes of *From Here To Eternity*.
Sinatra had pulled a face, wrinkled his nose and said simply,
'Nah!'

'Just you wait,' said Clift. 'They like comebacks.'

Now, as the run in to the Oscars began, Clift's words came
back loud and strong. Sinatra recalled Joan Crawford. Back in
the mid forties she'd been sacked by MGM because they
thought she was all washed up. She'd signed for Warners and
made *Mildred Pierce*. It won her an Oscar as best actress of the
year. Sinatra too had been sacked by MGM. It would be nice to
prove that they had also been wrong about him.

The eve of poll announcement by *Daily Variety* offered
reassurance. Its prediction was that *From Here To Eternity* would
be named best film and Fred Zinnemann best director. William
Holden was favourite for best actor for his POW Sefton in Billy
Wilder's *Stalag 17* and Audrey Hepburn was ahead as best
actress for her runaway princess in *Roman Holiday*. In the
supporting categories Sinatra and Donna Reed were both highly
fancied. *Variety*'s only word of caution was that Burt Lancaster
was closing in fast on Holden.

At Columbia Harry Cohn was already beginning to bubble. A
clean sweep, he announced confidently to the press. We'll win

more Oscars than any other studio.

Sinatra wasn't quite so sure. Daily, he cast his eyes over the other four actors in his category. They looked a pretty formidable bunch. Each time he picked a different winner. Jack Palance, for instance. He was nominated for his lethal gunfighter in the western *Shane*. It was Palance's second nomination. A year before he'd been nominated for trying to murder Joan Crawford in *Sudden Fear*. He hadn't won. Voters remembered such things. Palance could get it on the sympathy vote.

Then there was the 10-year-old Brandon de Wilde for his ranch boy in the same movie. Unlikely though as child performers didn't usually win competitive Oscars. The always reliable Eddie Albert was a greater threat. He was up for his freelance photographer in *Roman Holiday*, a film much favoured by Academy members. Lastly there was Robert Strauss, the surprise selection of the five. He had been named for his 'Dragfoot', the POW with a Betty Grable fixation in *Stalag 17*. Could be. No, thought Sinatra, not really. I must have a better chance. But then again ... The tension was relieved by Strauss himself. So delighted was he with his nomination that he printed his acceptance speech in advance in the trade papers. It encouraged him, amused Hollywood but didn't sway the voters.

The awards evening was on 25 March at the RKO Pantages Theatre. Word was out that next year Sinatra would be in contention for best song for *Three Coins In The Fountain* but in the early spring of 1954 singing was, for once, the last thing he had on his mind.

He arrived with his two children, Nancy jun. and Frank jun. They sat with him throughout the awards. It was a long wait. Unlike modern ceremonies, the supporting awards were not the first to be announced. The documentary awards came first, presented by Liz Taylor and her then husband Michael Wilding. Then came the sound and editing awards. Both went to *Eternity* – a good sign.

Costumes came next and Gene Tierney presented a deserved Oscar to Edith Head for *Roman Holiday*. Then there were the awards for colour costumes. This time, *The Robe*. The audience buzzed. The awards were splitting. Perhaps there would be no clean sweep after all. Harry Cohn began to feel uncomfortable.

Sinatra nervously wiped his palms. Frank jun. and Nancy jun. seemed transfixed.

Then suddenly *Eternity* was back on the map. Fred Zinnemann rose to collect the director's award and Donna Reed, looking beautiful and tranquil, found herself clutching the Oscar for best supporting actress. Sinatra next?

Mercedes McCambridge, award winner for *All The King's Men* and later to earn somewhat dubious acclaim as the voice of the devil in William Friedkin's *The Exorcist*, read out the nominees. To Sinatra her voice sounded more like that of an angel as she opened the envelope and announced, 'Frank Sinatra for *From Here To Eternity*.' Harry Cohn's clean sweep was coming true after all.

Sinatra grinned at his children, trotted to the stage, hugged host Donald O'Connor and kissed McCambridge. His smile went from ear to ear and then some. 'If I start thanking everybody I'll do a one-reeler,' he said amid laughter. 'They're doing a lot of songs up here tonight but nobody asked me.' He shrugged. The laughter mixed with applause. 'I love you though.' He walked off arm in arm with McCambridge.

Less than an hour later, *Eternity*'s triumph was complete. It received eight awards including best picture, the most won by a single film since the pre-war *Gone With The Wind* and all of them won by a film shot in the standard ratio without a gimmick of any kind – no CinemaScope, no 3D, no stereophonic sound, not even colour. Hollywood moguls, especially Zanuck, had been trying all of these things to attract audiences back to the cinema. They were left more than a little bewildered.

For Harry Cohn it was the biggest night of his career. It was more satisfying than when he'd won his first Oscar for *It Happened One Night*, more rewarding than when *All The King's Men* had taken best picture some four years earlier. All the arguments as to whether Sinatra should or should not have played Maggio became history. Cohn slapped Buddy Adler firmly on the back and made wild promises about future productions. Donna Reed remained in a trance. Zinneman took it quietly, savouring the moment. Daniel Taradash believed at last that he had written a worthwhile script. The only person not sharing in the festivities was the man who had perhaps the most to celebrate – Sinatra.

70

He ducked the party, lost the crowds and took a walk – Just him and his Oscar. As he ambled along the quiet, deserted streets of Beverly Hills he relived all the ups and downs, all the successes and failures of his career. Mostly now he remembered the good things. For the first time in several years he felt as though he was winning again.

His only mistake was forgetting that no one walked alone in Beverly Hills at night, especially movie stars, and especially those clutching a little gold statuette that was prized the world over. When a couple of motor cops pulled up alongside and asked him 'where he had got that thing he was carrying' he had more trouble explaining than he'd had with his acceptance speech. Luckily, one of the cops was a movie fan. He got out of the car, shook Sinatra's hand and assured his partner that, yes, this was the guy who just an hour or so before had won the Oscar and that the statuette had definitely not been stolen.

When he got back to his house, Frank rang his mother in New Jersey. He also rang Nancy. There was a cable from Ava. It read, 'Congratulations darling!' She too had been an Oscar nominee that night for *Mogambo*. It would be the only time she was ever nominated. She lost to Audrey Hepburn.

Sinatra said later that winning the Oscar was one of the greatest moments in his life and that it marked a turning point in his career. Quite where his career might have gone if he hadn't won on that March evening is anybody's guess but there was no doubt that, to the 30 million people watching the ceremony on TV, Sinatra was very definitely back. He quipped later: 'It was a dream that came true. It's quite a dream. I still have it three nights a week. I'd have it seven nights but I don't go to bed four nights a week.'

It was all a far cry from the desolate days of 1951 when Sinatra had sat by a phone that wouldn't ring, wondered what had happened to his so-called 'friends' and found out just how tough it was to borrow money when you were on the skids.

Hollywood Reporter columnist Mike Connolly offered a pompous warning not to allow the Oscar win to go to his head, 'We hope Sinatra realizes the enormous responsibility that comes with this kind of success.'

Reporters and journalists labelled their features 'The Greatest Comeback of All Time' and, for the first time, Sinatra began to grow angry and impatient with the word. Why 'comeback'? He'd never been away. When reporters added the tag 'lucky' he grew more restive still. 'Luck is fine,' he said in an interview, 'and you have to have luck to get the opportunity – in this case to get the role. But after that you've got to have the talent and know how to use it.'

They were not empty words. He was to prove his point many times in the months that lay ahead.

10   Young At Heart

'I want you to find the lousy bum and run
him off the lot and be sure he stays off
until this picture is in the can.'

Jack L. Warner

The question facing Sinatra in the Spring of 1954 was, should
he return to a major studio and a seven year contract or, like his
contemporaries, rely on taking one picture at a time and remain
independent?

British newcomer Richard Burton was one who had opted for
safety. He had signed a seven-picture deal at Fox at $100,000 a
picture. The films would be spread over seven years. They
would be chosen by his studio, not Burton. It was a good deal.
Burton though was twenty-eight. Sinatra was just two years
away from forty. He recalled his days at MGM. They had not
been happy ones.

It was Sinatra's musical commitments that eventually decided
the matter. His recordings and his night-club engagements
determined that he remained independent, especially as he had
now signed his new contract with Capitol Records. Movies had
become all-important after the Oscar win but the rule remained
– the films fitted in around his music, not the other way round.

Nonetheless, Sinatra was scarcely away from the cameras for
the rest of the year. He oiled the wheels with a four-week
quickie called *Suddenly* in which he played a would-be
presidential assassin, and he got together with another all-star
cast (Robert Mitchum, Olivia De Havilland, Gloria Grahame,
Broderick Crawford) in Stanley Kramer's version of the
best-selling *Not As A Stranger*.

The meatiest role though came from Warner Brothers in a remake (with music) of the 1938 hit *Four Daughters*. Sinatra was cast in the old John Garfield part of a cynical young songwriter and all-time loser who creates havoc when he descends on a small-town musical family and falls in love with one of the daughters. The film offered Sinatra the first chance to reprise a role already played on screen by another actor. His co-star was Warner's vibrant musical gal Doris Day.

It was Jack L. Warner himself who put the package together. He was a past master at reworking old studio material. More than any other studio head he made the most of what he had in his archives. His biggest triumph had been with the film *Tiger Shark*, a small-scale movie starring Edward G. Robinson in which Eddie had lost an arm during the course of the action. It was subsequently remade, scene for scene, in a lumberjack setting. This time the leading character lost not an arm but a leg. The third time round, the leading man was a lion tamer and once again lost an arm. When the scriptwriters pointed out in some triumph, that this was hardly original and that they were simply reverting to the first version of the story, producer Bryan Foy replied, 'Nonsense, he has two arms hasn't he?'

Tiger Shark was rumoured to have been remade as many as eleven times, even finding its way into a jungle setting with its hero a big game hunter. Just what part of his anatomy he had lost by then remains a mystery locked away forever in the dusty vaults of Warner Brothers.

At least the same fate didn't befall *Four Daughters*. It was made just the twice, the second time as *Young At Heart*, the title of Sinatra's new hit record. The canny Jack Warner never let anything get by him. He had noticed that March, 1954 had not only been Oscar month for Sinatra. It had also marked the occasion when he had enjoyed his first number one hit in eight years. The last time he had topped the charts had been in 1946 with 'Don't Fence Me In'.

The new hit was a sentimental little ballad written by Johnny Richards and Carolyn Leigh. Sinatra had recorded it the previous December and somewhat against his better judgement. He wasn't overkeen on the song. He tended to go along with Nat King Cole and others who had turned it down. New material though was thin on the ground and four years earlier he himself had said no to a song that Nat Cole had turned into an Oscar-winning hit – 'Mona Lisa'. Perhaps a shot at 'Young At Heart' might bring him the same kind of luck. He made the right decision. As well as becoming the title of his new movie the song returned Sinatra to his place as the nation's number one singer. It was also his first hit with arranger and composer Nelson Riddle.

The relationship between Warner and Sinatra fascinated those at the studio during the making of *Young At Heart*. The pair got along famously. Sinatra quickly discovered that it would be a very different kind of relationship to the one he had experienced with Louis B. Mayer. Warner was genial company. He made bad jokes, had a tasteless sense of humour and he smiled a lot. That was sometimes a dangerous sign. Many employees later reported that he had been smiling when he had fired them.

Many also found him the most treacherous and mean-minded of the Hollywood moguls. Flynn, Bogart and Bette Davis had all fought with him. Bogart and Flynn had actually been asked by Warner to pay *him* $100,000 to release them from their contracts when they wanted to branch out on their own. Lauren Bacall said about his bad jokes, 'His trouble was that he always wanted to boil everything down to the lowest common denominator.' Billy Wilder commented, 'Warner would have given everything he owned to be a stand-up comedian. He tried it all the time and the results were pathetic.'

With Sinatra though, Warner was always on the level. As a frustrated performer, he worshipped the great entertainers of his time, especially Jolson who had made *The Jazz Singer* at his studio back in 1927. Also Sinatra. He envied Sinatra his talent. He admired his self-confidence and cheeky arrogance. As far as Warner was concerned Sinatra could more or less write his own ticket. There hadn't been too many Oscar winners at his studio in recent years. Sinatra was treated like royalty.

Even when he was being difficult, which was often during the filming of *Young At Heart*, Warner took his side. Sinatra for instance, announced that he would not die at the end of the film. He had died in too many of his recent films. He'd rather stay alive in this one. The scriptwriters pointed out that Garfield had died in the original movie. It cut no ice. That was a different film. No amount of persuasion could shake him. Came the statement: 'Change the ending or I walk!' The ending was changed.

Shortly after filming had started, an impatient Sinatra stalked off the set saying he wouldn't return until the cinematographer had been replaced; he took too much time to light the set. The cinematographer wasn't just any old run-of-the-mill Hollywood cameraman. He was the Oscar-winning Charles Lang, a distinguished veteran who had worked with such directors as Henry Hathaway (*Lives Of A Bengal Lancer*), Billy Wilder (*Ace In The Hole*) and Fritz Lang (*The Big Heat*). He still took too long argued Sinatra. He insisted that Lang be replaced. Warner assigned another cinematographer.

Someone else Sinatra wanted off the set was Martin Melcher, the then husband of Doris Day and a man with a reputation of being one of the biggest hustlers in the business. His usual ploy was to take a $50,000 handout for each of his wife's pictures, insist on an associate producer credit and then take no further interest in the production. When he tried to induce Sinatra to include in the film songs he, Melcher, owned Sinatra saw red. He ordered him out of his dressing-room and declared that he would leave the movie if he ever ran across Melcher on set again. News of the trouble reached Jack Warner. He issued the order, 'I want you to find the lousy bum and run him off the lot and be sure he stays off until this picture is in the can. That's it! An order! Got it?' The order was carried out. Melcher was banned from the lot.

Yet, for all the camaraderie between mogul and star, *Young At Heart* was not the hit Jack Warner had hoped for. To his mind he had brought together all the right ingredients for a smash box-office hit or, in *Variety* parlance, a 'sockeroo'. It didn't work out that way. Despite the Sinatra-Day combination, a hit song as the title, some standards for Sinatra, some new numbers for Doris, and a fine supporting cast – Ethel Barrymore, Gig Young, Dorothy Malone – the picture came across as too sweet and too sugary. Sinatra was Sinatra, said the critics, and, in his laconic way, effective but he fell a long way short of the memorable sardonic misfit created by John Garfield some sixteen years earlier. As to the picture itself? *The Saturday Review* said tartly, '*Young At Heart* proves that Hollywood has not lost its knack of making indifferent new pictures out of good old pictures.' Others shared similar views. Warner could not even fall back on the familiar cry, 'The critics, what do they know? It's the public that really counts!' The picture was a long way short of the big grosser he had been hoping for. It failed to make the list of the top ten movie hits of the year and lagged behind the studio's more dramatic offerings, *Mister Roberts, Battle Cry* and *The Sea Chase*.

Where Warner miscalculated was in his belief that this kind of family movie, with its old-fashioned values still held good at the box office. A homely tale, set mostly in a luxurious house standing in a street of peach trees, its garden squared off by a low, white picket fence, it presented a small-town America that never remotely rang true to life. In the forties, during the war years, audiences had gladly accepted the escapism and the make-believe and films such as *Meet Me In St Louis* and *It's A Wonderful Life* had almost persuaded them that it was all for real. But by 1954 the roses round the door approach looked suddenly *passé*. A year later, at the same studio, James Dean would tear middle-class values apart in *Rebel Without A Cause*. Small-town America, especially as represented by *Young At Heart*, would never be the same again.

Still, there were at least some good things to savour. Sinatra, with his air of doomed pessimism, and Doris Day, as homely as blueberry pie, meshed well together, the songs were tuneful and Ethel Barrymore, as the tart, worldly wise aunt of the family, uttered endearing pearls of wisdom to Sinatra and others whenever the plot looked as though it was running out of steam.

To Ray Heindorf, the film's musical director, Sinatra and Day were the best musical stars he'd ever worked with. He'd been at the studio since the thirties and had seen all the Warner musical stars come and go. Sinatra and Day, both of them former dance-band singers and without an acting lesson between them, topped them all. He said,

> What people tended to forget when watching stars like Frank and Doris was how easy they made it all seem. Audiences used to take it all for granted. They would say, 'OK, they can sing a bit and act a bit. That's what they're paid to do. But it was never as easy as it looked.'

The question I always threw back at those who took that view was, 'If it's that easy, why is it that very few actors can sing and quite a lot of singers can act?' You've only got to check through your movie history to see how true that is. Frank and Doris? They're naturals. They could do both.

When it came to recording songs, well Doris, she did two takes and that was it. I'd rehearse the studio orchestra for about twenty minutes, starting at 1 p.m. Doris always liked to record at lunchtime. She'd come in at 1.20, record the song three times and leave at about 1.45. I'd then take a bit of take 1, take 2 and take 3. That's how we'd do it. Sinatra? He was even quicker. One rehearsal, one take, finis. Thank you very much.

He's lasted longer than any of them. On *Young At Heart* his voice was so good, as good as it has ever been. He was getting close to middle age and the voice had that slight middle age sound too. Wonderful sound. People complained later about his voice going. That was all nonsense. His huskiness is better than most people's good voices.

Early middle age suited Sinatra in *Young At Heart*. For the first time on screen, he came across as the disillusioned male, the guy who has been dealt a bad hand in life and who delights in taking out his self-pity on all around him. It was an image he would enjoy fostering as the years went by. Even in straightforward action movies his cynicism was never far from the surface. There was a slight touch of Bogie about him. Had Jack Warner ever decided (and knowing Warner it was not beyond the bounds of possibility) to remake *Casablanca* then Sinatra would have been more than acceptable as Rick Blaine.

As Barney Sloan in *Young At Heart* Sinatra was more than adequate and at times superb. An enduring image in the movie is of him sitting in a saloon, alone at night. The chairs are stacked. The waiter who is wiping down the bar wanders over with a coffee. Tinkling idly at the piano, the floor being slopped and washed around him, Sinatra moves easily into a rendering of 'Just One Of Those Things'. With his trilby perched nonchalantly on the back of his head, his tie loosened, a cigarette smoking in an ash tray besides him, he delivers two minutes of memorable Sinatra. It hardly matters that a sixty-piece Warner orchestra suddenly wells up from nowhere to accompany him. The mood is infectious, the song a classic, the voice and delivery perfect. The magic lasts long after the scene has passed. It was and remains one of the great Sinatra moments.

11   Goldwyn, Spiegel
and Brando

'Singing and dancing is only a question
of a little more projection.'

Sam Goldwyn

Sinatra had signed off for 1954 by taking a full-page
advertisement in the trade papers. The advertisement listed the
various awards he had received during the year. Then came the
films he had in release. Next the films he was currently shooting.
Then the one he was about to start in the New Year. He signed
the ad with a cocky, tongue-in-cheek flourish, 'Busy, busy, busy
– Frank'.

In the music world too he was back at the top. *Metronome*
named him best singer of the year and in *Downbeat*'s annual poll
of readers he was thousands of votes ahead of his nearest rivals,
Nat King Cole, Billy Eckstine, Eddie Fisher and Perry Como.
In its annual poll of disc jockeys, *Billboard* voted him the top
male vocalist, 'Young At Heart' the best single, and 'Swing
Easy' the top album.

It was the album, the new 10 inch (later 12 inch) LP that had
been his saviour. With its eight songs, four on each side, it freed
him at a stroke from the demands of having to concentrate on
finding one three-minute song that might make it into the
charts. The album offered up untold possibilities for his kind of
music. He could choose his own material, including standards,
and use backing arrangements by Nelson Riddle that enabled
him to develop a new swinging ballad style, a style that was at

80

times heightened by an exhilarating jazz-influenced spontaneity.

It was in the midst of all this welcome rebirth of popularity that Sinatra began occupying himself with landing a role in the film that everyone in Hollywood wanted to be a part of – Sam Goldwyn's screen version of the Broadway hit, *Guys And Dolls*. The show had run for 1,200 performances in New York and boasted fourteen hit songs by Frank Loesser. It was based on a Damon Runyon fable about two romances – one between Sky Masterson, a high-rolling gambler, and Sarah Brown, the young lady in charge of the Broadway branch of the Save-a-Soul Mission; the other between Nathan Detroit, proprietor of the oldest established permanent floating crap game, and his fiancée of fourteen years, Miss Adelaide, a brassy blonde who heads the floor show in a joint called the Hot Box!

Sinatra had his eyes firmly fixed on the Masterson role. He might have got it too had one of the top musical studios in town landed the rights. As it was, MGM, who were struggling and beginning to lose their musical dominance, could only go to $850,000. Paramount, Columbia and others had dropped out long before. It was left to Sam Goldwyn to land the prize with a million dollar bid, plus 10 per cent of the gross, the highest then paid for the screen rights of a Broadway musical.

The minute Goldwyn closed the deal Sinatra and other musical hopefuls instantly became also-rans. Goldwyn was an independent and idiosyncratic producer. He was also old-fashioned. He didn't like location work or too much realism in his pictures. The studio was where his films had always been made and the studio was where *Guys And Dolls* would be filmed.

He also firmly believed in going with the stars of the moment. Marlon Brando was the most acclaimed actor of the fifties. He would be his Sky Masterson. The fact that Brando couldn't sing was immaterial. Goldwyn claimed that Brando's acting talent was so great he could easily adapt to any sort of role. He added, 'Singing and dancing is only a question of a little more projection.'

Frank Loesser, perhaps realizing that many of his great songs were about to be ruined on screens across the world, did his best to sound positive. 'Brando's voice *is* untrained,' he admitted. 'But it has a pleasing, husky baritone quality.'

Brando didn't exactly help to inspire confidence when he

came out with the admission that the only real singing he had done had been in his bath and that in his opinion he had a voice that sounded like the mating call of a yak. It was an opinion with which Sinatra wholeheartedly concurred. It galled him that he would not be able to get his vocal chords around such Loesser songs as 'Luck Be A Lady'. It galled him too that this was the second time in just eighteen months that he had lost out to Brando.

The first occasion had been towards the end of 1953 when he had been kicking his heels at Fox on the abortive *Pink Tights*. Sam Spiegel had approached him to play the lead in a new picture he was having trouble getting off the ground. He needed a star name to give him a bit more clout. Sinatra was 'hot' after *From Here To Eternity*. Would he help them out? Sinatra agreed immediately. The film was right up his alley, a fierce controversial tale of corruption and violence among New York's longshoremen. Budd Schulberg had written the screenplay and Elia Kazan was set to direct. Sinatra's role was that of a slightly punch-drunk ex-boxer who rebels against and takes on the racketeers. The film would later become known as *On The Waterfront*.

Spiegel and Kazan reckoned they could get by on $900,000 and that they could shoot the movie on a thirty-five-day location schedule in New York. Not a single studio showed any interest, not even Fox where during the forties Darryl Zanuck had made something of a name for himself tackling such controversial subjects as anti-semitism and racial prejudice. That was then, he explained to Spiegel and Kazan, this is now, holding up his hands to the posters adorning his walls, all of them promoting CinemaScope films shot around the world. Spiegel and Kazan went away duly chastened. If not Zanuck, who?

The only man left to try was Harry Cohn at Columbia. He surprised them by saying 'yes'. *Eternity* had been a black and white movie without any frills. That had turned up trumps. Why not this one. Besides at $900,000 it was a snip. He had just one condition. No Sinatra. Instead, Brando. Spiegel and Kazan were amazed. *Eternity* had been a box-office smash. Sinatra had won the Oscar. He had been part of the film's success.

Cohn agreed but he didn't think that Sinatra could carry a role as demanding as Terry Malloy in *On The Waterfront*, at least, not yet. Brando was a different matter. He had enjoyed an unbroken run of critical successes that included *The Men, A Streetcar Named Desire, Viva Zapata!* and *Julius Caesar*. He had proved himself. Spiegel agreed, Sinatra was dropped, and Brando was signed.

The man most embarrassed by the volte-face was Kazan. He was so certain Sinatra had been signed that he was having script and wardrobe discussions with the actor when he learned he had been replaced. Sinatra was furious. He sued Spiegel for breach of contract and demanded $55,000 as compensation. When he encountered Spiegel in a restaurant the producer greeted him with, 'Hi Frank'.

Sinatra said curtly, 'You say hello Mr Sinatra. I prefer it if you don't say anything at all.'

A distraught Kazan wrote to Sinatra expressing regret that they would not, after all, be working together. It was months before Sinatra replied. When he did it was in a conciliatory manner. He wrote, 'For me to tell you that I was not deeply hurt would not be telling you my true feelings. However, with the passing of time and after re-reading your letter, how could I do or say anything other than I too want to be friends with you. I hope it's going well.' As Kazan commented, not a little shamefaced. 'Frank had let me off easy.'

No one who has seen Brando in *On The Waterfront* could conceivably believe that Sinatra would have been his equal, or even come close – nor any actor for that matter. Brando's performance remains one of the greatest ever seen on screen, a brilliant performer at the height of his powers interpreting to perfection one of the best screenplays ever written for an American movie.

Sinatra would, however, very definitely have made a better Sky Masterson. If he was bruised at being rejected for *On The Waterfront* he was devastated at being passed over for *Guys And Dolls*. The Loesser songs would have been second nature to him, the Runyonesque dialogue would have tripped easily from his lips, he would have been perfectly at home in the milieu of Times Square. Goldwyn, though, had made his choice.

All things considered Sinatra would have been best advised to cut his losses at this point and forget all about *Guys And Dolls*. There were plenty of other offers coming in, more than he could handle. What is more, Goldwyn seemed to be compounding his mistakes by casting yet another non-singer, Jean Simmons ('she was always half a tone off pitch,' according to a musical director on the film) and assigning a non-musical director, the Oscar-winning Joseph L. Mankiewicz to helm the movie. But such was the hype surrounding the film – that it was going to be a once in a lifetime experience, the best musical ever made, etc. – that Sinatra couldn't get the picture out of his mind. It stuck with him and refused to go away. He decided he'd rather be part of *Guys And Dolls* than miss it altogether. How about the secondary role of Nathan Detroit? Sam Levene had played it on Broadway. Mankiewicz would have liked him in his film. Sinatra on this occasion came in first. Goldwyn decreed that he be Nathan Detroit.

From the very start Sinatra and Brando did not get along. Their initial clash occurred during the very first week of shooting. They were required to share a long dialogue scene in Mindy's restaurant. Sinatra is desperate to raise money for a crap game. The bone of contention is whether Mindy's sells more cheesecake or strudel. Sinatra needs to get Brando to bet one way or the other. All the time he's talking he is eating mouthfuls of cheesecake.

The scene was wordy but not difficult. As usual Sinatra got it right first time, everything perfect. Brando, however, had trouble with the Runyon dialect and faltered over the words. Mankiewicz yelled 'cut' and they went for take two. Sinatra fretted. If he could get it in one take why the hell couldn't Brando?

Brando though was a method actor. He liked to explore, to dig deep into the inner motive of his character, to take his time. Take two was no better than take one. Sinatra's mood continued to darken. By take three he was seething. By take eight he exploded. He pushed the cheesecake to one side and snarled at Mankiewicz, 'These fucking New York actors. Who do they think they are? How much cheesecake do you think I can eat?'

If Mankiewicz had been considering a reply he should have delivered it a mite earlier. By the time he had opened his mouth Sinatra was already on the way to his dressing-room, still cursing Brando and the method and wondering why the fucking hell he'd wanted to be in this lousy movie in the first place. It took Mankiewicz a good half hour to get Sinatra to cool down and get him back on the set.

The plus side of things as far as Sinatra was concerned was that he didn't have to share too many scenes with Brando. Both actors worked in parallel sub-plots, Brando with Simmons and Sinatra with Vivian Blaine but when they did get together the tension was always palpable, always close to the surface.

Mankiewicz was the man in the middle, the peacemaker as well as the director. It was Brando's temperament he had to deal with next. After shooting had been in progress for a few weeks Brando suggested that Sinatra was playing his part all wrong. He told Mankiewicz that Sinatra was supposed to sing with a Bronx accent and clown things up more. He felt that Sinatra was singing like a romantic lead. 'And we can't have two romantic leads, can we,' he said softly. Brando waited.

Mankiewicz could see that he was expecting some kind of immediate decision. 'What do you suggest I do about it, Marlon?' he asked.

'Tell him,' said Brando.

Mankiewicz stared incredulously at his star. The actor was telling *him* to tell *Sinatra* how to sing a song. He smiled. 'You first,' he said and walked away. Brando was left fuming.

Sinatra's demeanour was not improved by the Oscar ceremonies that were held on 30 March, shortly after filming had started on *Guys And Dolls*. A year earlier he had been the one to bask in Oscar glory for his performance in *From Here To Eternity*. Now it was Brando who was in the limelight and for a film that had first been offered to Sinatra – *On The Waterfront*.

Brando was hot favourite. He had been nominated as best actor during the previous three years. Surely he would not fail this time. And so it proved. Best Actor for Terry Malloy! Things were made worse for Sinatra by the fact that tradition required he attend the ceremony to present the award for the best supporting actress. The winner was Eva Marie Saint, an actress he would himself have starred opposite had not Spiegel reneged on his deal. Sinatra didn't even bother to sing his Oscar nominated song, 'Three Coins In The Fountain'. It won but it was Dean Martin who performed it at the Pantages Theatre.

Sinatra's pet name for Brando during the filming of *Guys And Dolls* was 'Mumbles'. He asked Mankiewicz not to call him to the set until 'Mumbles' had finished his five-hour rehearsal. 'Then I'll give you what you want from me in 1½ minutes!'

By the end of filming things had become so fraught the two men hardly spoke to each other. Even such a simple event as arranging a photo-shoot for *Vogue* magazine proved to be a problem. Richard Avedon wanted a picture of Sinatra and Brando together. A simple enough request but not the easiest thing to arrange. Negotiations dragged on for days. Eventually it was agreed that the only time the two men could be photographed together was off-set on a Saturday morning. Even then there were problems. Neither man would come out of his dressing room before the other. 'Where's Frank?,' asked Marlon. 'I'll come out when he does.'

'Where's Marlon?,' asked Sinatra. 'I'll come out when he comes out.' In the end a publicity man arranged for a signal for Sinatra and Brando to emerge simultaneously. They smiled for the cameras. They looked at each other. They looked happy. They went through the motions again. Smiles, happiness, cordiality. Then back to the dressing-room and hostility.

The end result of all the hassle was as many had expected when Goldwyn had set about his bizarre casting – a mess. *Guys And Dolls* emerged as a Goldwyn circus that lurched around in all directions, always slightly out of control. In no way did it reflect the vigour and sparkling originality of its Broadway source. There was even a bump-and-grind number called 'Pet Me Poppa' that was especially written for the film to accommodate the latest bunch of Goldwyn Girls. Sinatra did get to sing one new song 'Adelaide' but for the rest of the time he was lost in chorus numbers such as 'Guys And Dolls' and 'Fugue For Tinhorns'. It wasn't a lot for the country's number one singer.

When he looked at the final cut of *Guys And Dolls* Mankiewicz knew that he didn't have a good picture. It stumbled and crawled when it should have bounced, the CinemaScope screen hindered rather than enhanced the action, the stylized sets of Oliver Smith kept the film in a kind of never-never land that didn't remotely resemble New York and there was no chemistry between any of the actors. The best thing in it was Vivian Blaine the only member of the leading quartet to have appeared in the original Broadway show. 'It was too slow, too talky,' said

Mankiewicz candidly.

He might also have added, 'Too dull' or to use a famous Goldwynism, 'It was more than magnificent, it was mediocre!'

What the film needed was a studio like MGM, a studio that was bursting at the seams with musical talent both before and behind the cameras, people such as: Minnelli, Walters, Donen, Gene Kelly, Cyd Charisse, Ann Miller. Any one of these would have helped turn *Guys And Dolls* into something quite memorable. The chance was missed because the studio could not afford to run to another $200,000.

The box-office take was just over $8 million, a poor return on an investment of over $5 million. Some critics made the right noises about the film but many were lukewarm. Neither Brando nor Sinatra came in for any special praise.

Brando's final summing up of the movie, 'It's hardly worth getting on your tricycle for.' And Sinatra? To this day at his concerts he cannot resist the dig when he prepares to sing 'Luck Be A Lady'. 'I made a movie once,' he says. 'And who did they get to sing this song? A bum who couldn't sing.' He then launches into three spellbinding minutes to prove his point that Sam Goldwyn made the worst decision of his career.

12   A Monkey on His Back

'One peddlar can ruin a lot of kids' lives.'
Frank Sinatra

The conversation went something along these lines, 'Frank, you interested in this drug thing, the one Preminger's playing about with?'

'*The Man With The Golden Arm?*'

'Yeah. Word's out that it's you or Brando.'

'Mumbles! *Again!*'

'Yeah, yeah …'

'Send me the script.'

'It's not finished. Preminger's only got fifty pages.'

'Send me what he's got.'

'OK, if you say so.'

The agent made contact. A day later the fifty pages arrived. Preminger played it straight down the line.

Fifty pages to each actor with an accompanying note apologizing for the fact that it was only a part script. The rest would follow as soon as it was available, probably in about three weeks.

The fifty pages told the first part of the tragic story of Frankie Machine, a low-life poker dealer trapped in the slums of Chicago with a crippled wife and a massive addiction problem. John Garfield had been the first to try to film Nelson Algren's sordid tale but had been unable to lick it into shape for the censor. After Garfield's premature death the rights passed to Preminger. He had no intention of appeasing the censor. He would release the film without the usual Production Code Seal

88

of Approval. Ten years earlier Billy Wilder had made *The Lost Weekend*, the first film to look seriously at the horrors of alcoholism. Now Preminger wanted to be the first film-maker to make the first serious film about drug addiction. Sinatra returned the fifty pages within twenty-four hours. 'Tell Preminger I'll do it,' he told his agent.

'You don't understand,' protested a bewildered Preminger. 'You will need to see the rest of the script. There have been changes.'

'He'll *do it*,' said the agent.

Sinatra was signed on the spot. It wasn't the speed of decision or Sinatra's obvious enthusiasm that helped Preminger to make up his mind. It was the vulnerability he had detected in Sinatra's character. He had been re-running some of Sinatra's movies. Sinatra seemed to be at his best when portraying men on a losing streak. Maggio in *From Here To Eternity* and Barney Sloan in *Young At Heart* had both been no-hopers at odds with the world around them. Frankie Machine was in the same mould: card-dealer, jail-bird, drug addict, an all-time loser. Preminger saw Sinatra as the perfect actor to bring him to life on screen.

Brando's agent was livid when he heard the news. He had decided to wait for the rest of the script before approaching his client. Brando hadn't seen any of the initial fifty pages. For once, Sinatra had come out ahead in his unofficial 'role duel' with the great method actor.

Preminger's plan for *The Man With The Golden Arm* was to start filming on 1 October and have the picture in the can by the end of the month. November would take care of the editing. Previews, if needed, would be held in early December and the film in the theatres by the end of the month. The speed would ensure that no smaller studio would steal a march on him and produce a low-budget quickie about the drug problem. It also meant that his film would be ready for the Academy Award ceremonies in March.

Everything about the set-up appealed to Sinatra. This was how he liked to work – fast, efficiently and economically. He shrugged off Preminger's reputation for being something of a volatile character with a 'so what, so am I!'.

Both men decided that the best way to get along would be to gently send each other up, to kid each other as often as possible.

Sinatra would sometimes click his heels and chide Preminger about his heavy Austrian accent. 'Yes, Herr Doktor,' he would reply to one of Preminger's commands. Failing that he would refer to him as Ludwig, a middle name that Preminger had long since dropped. Preminger, for reasons best known to himself saw Sinatra not as Frank but as 'Anatol'. The name belonged to a character in an early Arthur Schnitzler play. Preminger didn't explain his reasons but 'Ludwig' and 'Anatol' the pair became during filming.

Sinatra later claimed that Preminger was the only director who ever taught him anything about movie-acting. He said, 'Before Otto I had to pick up things for myself. I'd never had an acting lesson in my life. I only wish I had but Preminger was the man who had the patience to really explain to me what the character of the dope-taker was all about and how he felt he should be portrayed.'

Like Preminger, Sinatra was concerned as to why narcotics were not allowed to be discussed on screen. 'The system's crazy,' he said. 'Every manner of things have been seen in movies but about drugs everybody's supposed to stick his head in the ground.' His main reason for playing Frankie Machine was that he wanted to illustrate the dangers of drugs, especially to kids. He remembered the problem from his own youth in Hoboken, 'There were a couple of older guys on the block who acted kinda funny and later I found out they were on junk. In poor, tough neighbourhoods like that, one peddlar can ruin a lot of kids' lives.'

The drug scenes in *The Man With The Golden Arm* were the most challenging of Sinatra's career. There were three of them, all strategically placed in the picture, one at the beginning, one in the middle and one at the end. The climax was the scene which caused all the publicity with Sinatra locked in his room and writhing and screaming as he goes 'cold turkey' and tries to kick the habit once and for all. The early scene was harrowing but brief, showing Sinatra caught in a jail with a screaming junkie. The few minutes in the middle of the picture were the most dramatic as Sinatra finally succumbs once more to the fix that will rid him, at least for an hour or two, of all the problems surrounding him in his suffocating world.

The scene develops slowly. It begins with the pusher (Darren

McGavin), drinking quietly at a bar, catching sight of Sinatra's controlled anguish in the mirror in front of him. The reflection shows Sinatra, his eyes wide and staring, nervously wiping the back of his hand across his drying mouth. McGavin smiles. He knows he has his man. Elmer Bernstein's music score begins to throb on the soundtrack. McGavin, whirling his cane in a dandyish, joyous fashion, heads off across the street to his apartment. He does not look back. He knows Sinatra will follow.

In his room McGavin methodically goes about his lethal preparations.

'Five bucks.'

'Last time it was two.'

'They keep raising the price on me.'

Sinatra does not argue. He rolls up his sleeve. McGavin, slow, cool, deliberate, prepares the syringe. He smiles, 'The monkey's never dead, dealer. The monkey never dies. When you kick him off he just hides in the corner, waiting his turn.'

The needle pierces the skin. Sinatra's eyes, wide in huge close-up, wince and briefly flicker. Bernstein's music rises to a crescendo. The eyes cloud over. The screen fades to black.

As a scene it was dynamite. Nothing like it had ever been seen before. Preminger had broken the rules in the most dramatic way possible. He had shown the actual drug-taking in clinical detail.

Sinatra, full of self-loathing, is superb. McGavin as the pusher is his equal, a forerunner of Frog One (Fernando Rey) in *The French Connection* and, like Rey, elegantly dressed – smart hat and jacket, a neat handkerchief in his top pocket, his shoes smartly polished, a cane across his arm. Not for him the squalor and misery of the lower depths but the financial gain to be made from the lower depths.

Audiences paid more than $4 million to see *The Man With The Golden Arm*. Quite whether they liked what they saw is debatable. The critics certainly weren't that impressed. In their view Preminger had treated the subject hysterically. He had gone for sensation. He had dramatized the drug scenes at the expense of the rest of the story. He had painted a convincing portrait of the Chicago slums, a seedy urban sub-world of sordid apartments, dimly lit backrooms and alleyways and shady nightspots, but he hadn't really got across the tragedy of Frankie Machine.

In Algren's original novel, Machine had been a Polish-American veteran of World War II, who returns to Chicago with a Purple Heart and a morphine habit and who tries to pick up his life as a stud-poker dealer in a gambling club. Unable to come to terms with his environment or kick his addiction, he eventually commits suicide.

In Preminger's film he became simply a guy with a drug problem who successfully throws off the habit. To soften things even further, Preminger even gave the film a happy ending with Machine starting a new life with his girlfriend.

Algren came out publicly against the film. He said that Preminger had done damage to his book. He also added that Preminger should have retained him to write the screenplay as had originally been agreed. Algren worked for just a few days on the script before Otto fired him. Preminger, who was never overkeen on authors adapting their own work, replaced him with professional screenwriter Walter Newman.

Preminger had originally promised Algren $1000 a week for four weeks' work on *The Man With The Golden Arm*. In the end, Algren had to fight through his agent, to get his expenses paid, something that was especially galling to him as Preminger was paying Sinatra $100,000 plus 10 per cent of the film's profits. He said, 'I've borrowed off a pickpocket and stolen a ten-spot from a whore and never had a pang of conscience but taking dough off Otto Preminger is something the normal stomach can't stand.'

He also went on record with his feelings about Hollywood in general, 'I went out there for a thousand a week and worked Monday. I got fired on Wednesday. The fellow who hired me was out of town Tuesday.'

Preminger dismissed Algren's vitriol. He had suffered similar problems with authors before. Vera Caspary had been most unhappy with what he had done with her classic murder mystery *Laura*. And there had been others. He said:

> What authors don't understand is that when the contract says it 'sells' the rights to the book it means just that. After that, I, or any other director can do what we want with the material. I don't think I did an injustice to Algren's book. I had been acquainted with it for a long time. I knew the characters well.

Preminger added that he wanted to stress in the film the problem of taking drugs 'just for fun!'. He said:

> *That* is what I wanted to emphasize, that people think they can take it for kicks as they call it and suddenly leave it alone. As Frankie says in the picture, 'I thought I could take it or leave it and suddenly I noticed that I couldn't leave it anymore' – *there* is the danger. I also tried to show in the picture that the psychological cause is really what keeps the man on narcotics. The physical cure is comparatively easy today if you take it in hospital with the help of drugs and doctors. But the psychological cure is very hard. Statistics show that people fall back into the habit in alarmingly high numbers, because of mental unhappiness.

As for his decision to defy the censor and show narcotics on screen? 'A lot has been made of it. I've always taken the view that exposing a sore is much better than hiding it.'

Sinatra came out of things better than the picture as far as the critics were concerned. He also earned his first best actor Oscar nomination for his role. One notice that gave him particular satisfaction was the one written by the esteemed Arthur Knight in the *Saturday Review*. Knight said:

> The thin, unhandsome one-time crooner has an incredible instinct for the look, the gesture, the shading of the voice that suggests tenderness, uncertainty, weakness, fatigue, indeed despair. He brings to the character much that has not been written into the script, a shade of sweetness, a sense of edgy indestructibility that actually creates the appeal and intrinsic interest in the role ... He is an actor of rare ability, it is a truly virtuoso performance.

For Preminger, Sinatra was just about the perfect movie-actor. He was quick, he was professional, he learned fast. They only had one small tiff when Sinatra wanted to fire the chief electrician because, in his opinion, he had not done his job properly. Preminger took him aside and said quietly that on his pictures he was the one who did the firing. The technician stayed.

Years later, Paramount offered Preminger *The Godfather*. Preminger was one of many directors to consider it. He felt that

Sinatra would be wonderful as Don Vito Corleone. He put the offer to Frank. He even offered to eliminate the character of the singer who some people thought was patterned after Sinatra. Sinatra simply cabled him, 'Ludwig. I pass on this.'

Preminger told Paramount that he didn't want to do the film without Sinatra so he passed. When the film eventually went before the cameras in 1972 Francis Ford Coppola was at the helm. Playing the Mafia Chief, Don Corleone? Marlon Brando!

13 Songs for Swinging Movies

'I opened the Cole Porter lyric book and found this song called "Well Did You Evah?" It was so perfect.'

Saul Chaplin

In every movie he offered a glimpse of something new. Sometimes it was just a look, a glance even, but always it was held long enough to have the most unsettling effect. On other occasions it was the pain in the eyes, the hurt and the little twitch of nervousness as he realized he had overstepped the mark.

Then there was the world-weary, laconic delivery, especially effective when he was being cynical and so persuasive it made one regret he had never played Hemingway. Most characteristic of all, perhaps, was the flash of anger, sudden and dangerous, as he exploded into violence.

At the other end of the scale there was the lighter, playboy side, enhanced as always by the wide grin, the laughter as well as the song in the voice, the wisecracks effortlessly timed. Few stars of the fifties offered such a potent mix. Audiences responded the world over. In 1956, for the first time in his career, Sinatra was voted one of the world's top ten moneymaking movie stars.

Just about the only thing he couldn't come up with was the thing that audiences wanted from him the most: an ongoing sequence of hit film songs. In the early fifties, other singers – Doris Day, Dean Martin, Mario Lanza, Rosemary Clooney – had laid claim to those. Sinatra had to be content with 'Three

95

Coins In The Fountain' which, as he was the first to admit, had been something of a fluke, a case of being in the right place at the right time.

It was with *The Tender Trap* that Sinatra at last got into top gear. The film brought him back to MGM. It was the first time he had been at Culver City since he had sung and danced with Gene Kelly and company in *On The Town*. This time things were different. There was no dancing in *The Tender Trap*, just singing and then only behind the opening and closing credits. There was also no playing second fiddle to Gene or any of the other dancing stars. In *The Tender Trap, Sinatra* was the star, a playboy theatrical agent who meets his match in the form of a persistent young woman (Debbie Reynolds) who is so determined to get a husband she even has a timetable for catching one. The film was bright and breezy and witty. It derived from a Broadway show and at times betrayed its origins but it became a hit primarily because of its superb title song which remained in the charts for four months and earned Jimmy Van Heusen and Sammy Cahn an Academy Award nomination. It came close on Oscar night but lost to the somewhat less bouncy song about *amour*, 'Love Is A Many Splendoured Thing'.

If *The Tender Trap* was basically a comedy with a hit song tagged on for good measure, *High Society* was the genuine article, a musical version of the 1940 hit *The Philadelphia Story*. The plot was basically the same as the original: a spoiled society heiress, about to marry for the second time, is thrown into turmoil when her former husband turns up at the wedding along with a couple of reporters who are covering the occasion for their less than reputable *Spy* magazine. Grace Kelly, in her last screen role, played the heiress, Bing Crosby the former husband and Sinatra and Celeste Holm the reporters. The only change was in the locale, the action being moved from Philadelphia to Rhode Island so as to incorporate the Newport jazz festival and allow for the welcome appearance of Louis Armstrong and his Band.

MGM paid Cole Porter $250,000 to write nine original songs for the movie. It was money well spent. Porter knew the milieu. He came up with something for just about everyone: 'Now You Has Jazz' for Crosby and Satchmo; the romantic 'True Love' for Crosby and Kelly; 'You're Sensational' for Sinatra; and the evergreen 'Who Wants To Be A Millionaire?' sung by Sinatra and Celeste Holm as they jig skittishly around a table piled high with expensive wedding presents. The other songs were of similar quality.

Just one song defeated him: the one the studio and eventually, the audience, wanted to hear the most – the duet between Crosby and Sinatra. The pair had never sung together on screen. Sinatra recalled how ten years earlier he had gazed across from RKO to the Paramount lot and vowed that one day he would be the equal of his idol. Now, here he was, about to sing with him for the first time, or so he thought, and no song. Try as he might Porter could find no way of including in his score a duet for Crosby and Sinatra. MGM cabled him to try again. Porter disliked defeat as much as anyone. Again he went over the script. Still nothing. Crisis!

It was the film's musical director Saul Chaplin who solved the problem:

> We knew we *had* to have a song for them to do together. There was no way we could make the picture without it. When Cole couldn't come up with one I began looking around for songs that Cole had already written, either for the stage or the movies. It didn't really matter which. All I knew was that we had to have something. By chance, I came across a song called 'Did You Evah?' It had been written by Cole for a show called *DuBarry Was A Lady* and we decided to put it in the picture when we couldn't come up with an original song.
>
> I know why Cole had trouble. For a song to really work in a picture there has to be something dramatic forcing you to do that kind of song. There was nothing like that in this picture. Frank and Bing were at this party in Newport. They wander into a room that has a bar and they both pour themselves a drink. Well, what is that? By accident, as I say, I opened the Cole Porter lyric book and found this song called 'Well did you evah, what a swell party this is'. It was so perfect.

So too was a song that Sammy Cahn and Jimmy Van Heusen wrote for the 1957 Sinatra movie *The Joker Is Wild*. The film provided Sinatra with his most dramatic role since *The Man With The Golden Arm*. The role was that of a man Sinatra had known personally for a number of years, entertainer Joe E.

97

Lewis, a former saloon singer who, in the twenties, had his vocal chords slashed when he fell foul of gangsters and then made a comeback to become one of America's most sardonic night-club performers. His act wasn't to everyone's taste but it earned him a reputation in nightspots across the country. His speciality was to stand, or slightly sway, with a glass in one hand and offer slightly inebriated views on the things that go to make up everyday living. On drinking: 'I'm so glad many of my friends are here tonight, plus a few sober ones as well.' On ageing: 'An old man is somebody who can't take "yes" for an answer.' On gambling: 'If Paul Revere had been riding the horse I'd backed we'd all still be talking with a British accent.'

The sour humour even found its way into the part of the film that dealt with Lewis's personal life and his love affair with the bottle. When his doctor tells him that he will die a middle-aged man unless he gives up drinking he shrugs ruefully, 'I guess I can quit drinking. It shouldn't be too tough. I've done it a hundred times before.'

Critics began talking about another Oscar nomination for Sinatra. Not so Sinatra himself. He saw an Academy Award all right but not in his performance. He saw one in the film's theme song, 'All The Way'. After the film's première in Las Vegas, he called the film's musical director Walter Scharf in a state of high excitement. A half-asleep Scharf did his best to concentrate on what was being said at the other end of the telephone.

'Walter, you awake?'

'Frank?'

'The preview of *The Joker* was a smash!'

'That's great Frank. You rang to tell me *that*! For God's sake, it's way past midnight. Couldn't it have waited until morning?'

'There's an Oscar in the picture, Walter.'

'All The Way?'

'Yeah. Walter, trust me. I have a feeling about this. See what you can do about getting it into the picture a few more times. Do it any way you like but we gotta make the song more important. If it registers, it'll be a big hit. Take my word for it. Now go to sleep.'

Scharf didn't argue. Both he and Sinatra shared the same views about the song and Sinatra was obviously now past enthusiasm and into ecstatic about its potential. On the

Paramount lot Scharf looked again at *The Joker Is Wild*. He remixed part of the soundtrack, emphasizing the song both vocally and instrumentally throughout the movie – briefly on a record playing in a hotel bedroom, as a dance number played orchestrally at a charity benefit, as background music linking scenes.

He did his job well. Sinatra was spot on with his prediction. 'All The Way' duly won the Oscar as the best movie song of 1957. Later, whenever he met up with Scharf, Sinatra would smile, wrinkle his nose and point a finger at his arranger. 'See, what did I tell you. I know about these things Walter.'

What he didn't know about, however, was something called 'CinemaScope 55' and that simple fact alone marred what were otherwise golden years of movie songs for Sinatra.

CinemaScope 55 was the process that Darryl Zanuck planned to use to film his two big musicals of 1956: *The King And I* and *Carousel*. Sinatra had put it about that he very much wanted to be part of *Carousel*. The role of carnival barker Billy Bigelow would, he felt, be ideal for his talents. Zanuck had been looking to use Sinatra again every since the débâcle of *Pink Tights*. He signed him immediately. The deal was $150,000 for a ten-week shoot. Shirley Jones who had recently scored a big success in the film version of *Oklahoma* was cast as the female lead and veteran film-maker Henry King set to direct.

Sinatra arrived at the Booth Bay location in Maine in August of 1955. He was in good spirits. The fact that the film was going to be photographed in something called 'CinemaScope 55' didn't worry him in the least. To him it was just another wide-screen process. Hell, they were playing around with all kinds of screens and techniques these days. So this was another one. Let's get going. Time's money.

CinemaScope 55, however, was rather more than just another wide-screen technique. It was something Zanuck was banking on to improve the photographic quality of his CinemaScope productions. It meant shooting scenes in a 55 mm negative for added sharpness of image and then, for theatres not equipped for the bigger ratio, reducing the negative to 35mm for general release. There was just one problem. The process was in the experimental stage. Zanuck was unsure as to whether CinemaScope 55 would reduce satisfactorily to 35. He decided to play it safe. He would shoot the film in two versions – one in 55mm and the other in the normal 35mm he had been using for all his CinemaScope productions since 1953.

The news came like a thunderbolt to Sinatra. 'You mean I'm going to have to film each scene *twice*?,' he exclaimed in disbelief.

'That's the way Darryl wants it Frank. I guess we have no option.'

'No way. I signed to make one movie. If that's not gonna be the case I'm outa here!' Sinatra turned on his heel and headed for the dressing room. 'Get it sorted out or I'm off this picture. If you think I'm going to shoot each set up once, then hang around while they change all the cameras and shoot the scene again you're crazy.'

And with that production of *Carousel* stalled before a camera had even turned. The 125 strong cast and crew had nothing to do but sit and wait as the Fox representatives, Sinatra's lawyers and agent went into a huddle to try and sort things out. Neither side would budge. After a day, members of the company opted for sunbathing and making idle bets as to whether Frank would stay or walk. Those who plumped for a walk-out collected the money. After two days Sinatra's patience snapped. He decided he had had enough and walked off the picture. Ten days later he was replaced by Gordon MacRae.

Zanuck, who was now beginning to wonder just what he had to do to get Sinatra on screen in a Fox movie, threatened to sue for a million dollars. Sinatra stood his ground. For him it was a matter of principle. He likened it to the hiring of musicians. When they played on a sound stage for a movie their work couldn't be used on records without them being paid again. Therefore why should an actor make two films for the price of one which is exactly what he thought he was doing. He said: 'I'm not talking about the use of two cameras. That doesn't bother me. They can shoot any scene with as many cameras as they want, and they do. What I'm talking about is *playing* the same scene twice.'

Zanuck backed off. Many felt that Sinatra had a strong case. Besides, thought Zanuck, he might want to use Sinatra again some day. Ironically, just a few weeks later Zanuck's technicians revealed that the CinemaScope 55 process would reduce perfectly well and that there would be no need to film the picture twice over.

Sinatra's reaction is not on record but he must have had cause to regret that because of CinemaScope 55 and his own lack of patience he never got to sing Rodgers and Hammerstein on screen. For Sinatra fans it was one of the biggest disappointments of the fifties.

Ken Darby, Sinatra's old buddy from the RKO days and along with Alfred Newman, the man in charge of the music arrangements for *Carousel* remembered just how good Sinatra would have been in the picture. He said:

> Frank was working hard at the time, recording albums, playing club dates and so on, and I thought that his voice sounded a little strange, a little on the strained side. I mentioned this to him and suggested that perhaps he should vocalize which was something he didn't really like doing.
>
> [Darby laughed] Neither did he go much for my suggestion that his voice sounded a bit rough around the edges but after a while he seemed to come round and he vocalized a lot in preparing for the picture. That was unusual for Frank but he was determined to get into shape.
>
> He recorded just one song for the movie before he went on location – 'If I Loved You' and I can tell you his voice had never sounded so good. It was a sensational recording. MacRae was excellent in the movie but Sinatra would have been something else, a knockout. It was just a shame things didn't work out.

Carousel wasn't the only Sinatra disappointment of the mid fifties. Someone wrongly advised him that he could play a cowboy in *Johnny Concho* and a Spanish peasant in the epic *The Pride And The Passion*. He couldn't. Both were dismal failures.

The only other bright spot of the period was one that many people tend to forget. Any mention of *Around The World In Eighty Days* tends to conjure up memories of David Niven or Shirley MacLaine or Robert Newton. The forty odd guest stars tend to fade into the background. Sinatra was one of the guest stars. He appeared towards the end of the picture, in a Barbary Coast saloon decorated by Marlene Dietrich and run by tough-talking George Raft. All Sinatra had to do was play the piano. As he tinkles away to the tune of 'Them Golden Slippers' the camera focuses on his fancy black and yellow waistcoat, the garters clinging tightly to his white-shirted arms and the black derby perched on the back of his head.

Only when David Niven leaves the saloon does he deign to look round, a cigarette dangling from his mouth, a faint smile around his lips. Then he turns and goes back to the piano. His face is seen for approximately ten seconds. He arrived for filming mid morning and had long gone by lunch. That was how he liked 'em!

14   Pinewood and Lee J.

> 'Generous guy. Never accepted any
> money from me. Wouldn't take it. I guess
> we were just soul mates for a while.'
>
> Lee J. Cobb

As yet I have not intruded my presence in this biography other
then to quote from interviews I have enjoyed with those who
worked with and knew Sinatra. There is, however, one occasion
that I believe is worth recalling, one that illustrates a surprising
and little-known side of Sinatra's personality. The occasion was
when I was asked to visit Pinewood Studios to profile the
American actor Lee J. Cobb.

Cobb was in England to make a so-so comedy called *That
Lucky Touch*. His co-stars were Roger Moore, Susannah York
and Shelley Winters. His role was that of a cigar chomping
NATO general mixed up in arms dealing, war games and
marital mishaps in Brussels. He put out the line that it had
always been his ambition to play broad comedy but its doubtful
whether he really meant it. Tough racketeers, cynical newspaper
editors and downtrodden salesmen were what Cobb was all
about.

He was still wearing his army uniform when we lunched in
Pinewood's magnificent panelled dining-room. It was one of
those perfect but infrequent English summer days, warm with
broken sunshine and a slight breeze. Beneath the window the
lawns stretched out towards the row of tall hedges where Lotte
Lenya had once slammed a pair of knuckledusters into the solar
plexus of Robert Shaw in *From Russia With Love*. All around
were memories of films past. Inside, the conversation was all

films – what was happening now, what was happening next, who would get such and such a role, would the British film industry survive its latest crisis.

Cobb and I rambled pleasantly through a lazy lunch and a bottle of wine. We talked of his work on stage, especially his brilliant Willy Loman in *Death Of A Salesman*, his personal life, his political problems with the Un-American Activities Committee, and his films.

He grimaced at the mention of the films. That day it seemed everyone had asked him about his most famous screen role, the racketeer Johnny Friendly in Kazan's *On The Waterfront*. He seemed tired of it. I let it go.

How about *How The West Was Won*? He shrugged and said, 'Cowboys and Indians on a wide screen!' *Exodus*? 'Cowboys and Indians in Palestine on a wide screen!' His gangster boss in *Party Girl*? 'OK, I guess, a variation on Johnny Friendly. It didn't take a lot of work. I just shouted a lot.'

We carried on through them, *Coogan's Bluff* with Clint Eastwood, *Twelve Angry Men*, *The Brothers Karamazov*, *The Three Faces Of Eve*, the TV series *The Virginian* that eventually made him a household name and a wealthy man, and even *The Exorcist*. He shook his head at the mention of that film. 'People tend to forget I was ever in that film. I played the cop. All I had to do was snoop around and ask people questions. I wasn't around when they filmed the horror scenes. When I saw what they came up with … it didn't seem like the same movie.'

More as an afterthought than anything else I mentioned the film of Neil Simon's *Come Blow Your Horn*. It had been made in the early sixties and was about a young man's initiation into his playboy brother's swinging New York life style. I had expected it to be dismissed with an 'Oh, well,' but surprisingly it struck a chord. Cobb laughed, 'I played Sinatra's father in that … can you believe it … quite a guy our Frank, quite a guy.'

Was it true about his liking for quick takes? 'True!' roared Cobb. 'If you didn't get there early you missed the guy. I mean, man he was gone, like a rabbit.' He paused, 'There were three words I said to him over and over again in that movie, "You're a bum!" If I said it once I said it twenty times.' He shook his head. 'I can tell you, in real life he was anything but that.'

Cobb had slipped into reflective mood. He sipped his coffee

and gazed casually across the dining-room to see if there were any faces he recognized. He waved a 'hello' to director Edward Dmytryk who was sitting a few tables down the room. Dmytryk held up his hand in acknowledgement.

I pushed gently about Sinatra. Cobb puffed on his cigar. 'It's a funny thing about Frank – the stories people tell, about his temper, his bad connections, all that kind of thing. I never saw any of that.'

This was on *Come Blow Your Horn?*

'Before that, back in the fifties when the political business was on. You know, McCarthy and all that. A lot of people shunned me for naming names. I understand that. I wasn't proud of myself. I knew a lot of people were finding things difficult. Then came my heart attack. I was going through a divorce at the time ... I guess it must have been the strain. No money coming in, two sons to bring up.' He continued, 'Anyway I was in hospital and the doctors put it on the line. "You haven't had a big coronary," they said, "you've had a *massive* one." Their answer to things: "Complete rest and no worry." '

Cobb gave me the sly grin-cum-grimace I'd seen so many times on screen. 'No *worry*! God knows I couldn't act, couldn't even move and they said no worry. Anyway it was then that Frank arrived, right out of the blue.

'I tell you, he was the last person I'd expected to see. I'd only made one movie with him and that had been a piece of nonsense called *The Miracle Of The Bells*. He'd played a priest. I'd played a Hollywood producer. Perfect miscasting on both counts. That had been seven years before. I'd hardly seen him since.'

Was there a reason for the visit, I asked.

'Yeah, simply to pay my bills. Anything over and above the insurance he paid for – everything. Moved me into a rest home in the hills above L.A., then into his own home. Bought me books and flowers, anything you could think of. He did it all. He visited every day and every day I kept wondering why he was there.

'I started to ask him once but he got embarrassed and shut me up. He simply changed the subject. I do remember him telling me that he thought I should have won the Oscar for *On The Waterfront*. I didn't realize until later that he'd been in line for Marlon's part. Interesting that ... might have worked.'

What happened once you'd recovered, I asked.

'Nothing, that's the strange thing. The relationship just tapered off. He had things to do. My career was picking up again. Our paths didn't cross. As soon as he saw he could be of no further use he just kind of faded away. When we met again on the set of *Come Blow Your Horn* it was eight years on. No one would have known that I owed the guy my life. We had some pleasant times. It was an easy picture to make but it was no different to any other movie. Shot quickly, you know, hello-goodbye, that sort of thing.'

Cobb paused. 'Generous guy. Never accepted any money from me. Wouldn't take it. I guess we were just soul mates for a while. He'd been down and very nearly out. He knew what it was like to be down to your last dollar.'

He gave a huge laugh and in a stroke shook off the past. He got up to leave. 'It was all a long, long time ago.' I started to rise but he put his hand on my shoulder and said, 'Finish your coffee'. As he straightened his tie and picked up his general's hat he added, 'You know the thing I most regret about knowing Frank? That the two pictures we made together were so lousy.' He shook hands. 'Nice talkin' to you.' And with that he was gone – a warm, friendly, gentle man.

Fourteen months later he was dead, from a heart attack in New York, aged 62. I scanned the obituaries in the papers. They gave no indication as to whether Sinatra might have sent flowers. But my hunch was that he had.

15   Pal Joey

'I want Sinatra. If he plays Joey I'll sign
right away.'

Marlene Dietrich

Columbia boss Harry Cohn hadn't even considered Sinatra for
the part. For him *Pal Joey* had always been Gene Kelly. He had
been Joey on Broadway. He would repeat the role on screen.
And he would repeat it opposite Columbia goddess Rita
Hayworth. That was the plan. It didn't happen. 'Goddam
movie,' cursed Cohn. 'Should never have bought the thing. It's
unfilmable!'

'It was your decision Harry,' said his long-time friend
screenwriter Sidney Buchman. 'I know it was,' yelled Cohn.
'Don't remind me.' For once he had no one to blame but
himself.

In Hollywood, Cohn's purchase of the screen rights of *Pal
Joey* quickly became known as 'Cohn's Folly'. Those close to the
studio boss would occasionally taunt him with the words, 'When
are you going to film *Pal Joey* Harry?' Cohn would glare, utter an
expletive and then go on to discuss his next production.

The reason for all the problems lay in the musical's morality
or rather the lack of it. *Pal Joey* was a heel, an unscrupulous
night-club entertainer who ditches the girl who adores him so
that he can take up with a wealthy married woman who, in
return for sexual favours, promises to set him up in his own
night-club *Chez Joey*. Things go wrong. Ambition and greed get
the better of him. In the end he is left as he was at the beginning,
looking for the break that will never come and having ruined the

107

lives of those around him. The musical had a sharp, witty score by Rodgers and Hart and derived from a series of letters written for the *New Yorker* by John O'Hara. Each letter was signed, 'Your Pal Joey'.

Cohn's problem was that in the mid-forties the production code was stiff to the point of rigidity. Censorship was so tight there was no way that Joey's activities could be convincingly portrayed on screen. Cohn, who had planned the film as a successor to his hugely popular *Cover Girl* (which had also teamed Kelly and Hayworth) had no option but to put the property on ice. He concentrated instead on other musicals, *The Jolson Story* and *Jolson Sings Again*. Their success at the box-office at least went some way to compensating for what he believed was the most serious mistake of his career.

Director Billy Wilder was one of the first to convince him that it might just be possible to get *Pal Joey* off the ground. He told Cohn that he saw the film as a kind of musical variation of his Hollywood story *Sunset Boulevard* in which a much younger man had also been kept by an older woman. He wouldn't mind having a crack at the story. Was Cohn interested? Cohn was interested in anything that would get his long dormant musical on to the screen. He invited Wilder to dine with him at Columbia. Wilder put forward the suggestion that Joey be recast as a drummer and that Marlon Brando should play the lead. Mae West, he said, would be ideal for the older woman.

It didn't sound much like *Pal Joey* to Cohn but he agreed to give it a go. Wilder moved into the Columbia offices with his typewriter. He stayed for ten days and then left. He was unable to lick the story and rework it into his own concept. It was the only time in his career that he had worked at Columbia. He never returned. Two weeks after his departure he received what he thought was a note from Harry Cohn, thanking him for his efforts. There was no thank-you note in the envelope. Just a bill for two lunches. Price: $5!

After Wilder there were others who ran ideas past Cohn. A Columbia executive suggested doing *Pal Joey* as an all black musical. *Carmen Jones* had been a smash. It might be worth a try. The idea was dismissed. Then someone said how about Kirk Douglas. He had made a successful career out of playing heels. Cohn recalled films like *Champion, Ace In The Hole* and *The Bad*

108

And The Beautiful. He liked the idea. 'Great,' he said. 'Kirk's a fine actor. Let's talk!'

'He can't sing Harry,' reminded an aide.

'Forget it!' snapped Cohn.

Marlene Dietrich's name also came up. She was 56. She would be ideal as the woman who bankrolls Joey. Cohn was tempted. Dietrich wasn't exactly box-office but if the actor playing opposite her was a big enough star the combination might be intriguing. Tentative enquiries were made. Dietrich was not averse to the idea. It was she who first brought Sinatra's name into the casting game. 'I'll do it,' she said. 'But on one condition. I want Sinatra. If he plays Joey I'll sign right away.'

'He doesn't talk to me since *From Here To Eternity*,' said Cohn glumly. 'He won't do it.'

'No deal,' said Dietrich.

Cohn tried a last gambit. 'How about a young actor who's just coming up on the Columbia lot?'

'Who's that?'

'Jack Lemmon.'

'He's a nobody.'

End of discussion.

In the end it was director George Sidney who decided to pursue things with Sinatra. He had known Frank since they had filmed *Anchors Aweigh* together at Metro. He had since moved over to Columbia to try and bolster the studio's musical image with a series of independent productions. *Pal Joey*, it was hoped, would be one of them. Over a drink one night he brought Sinatra's name up once again. 'Harry, you know as well as I do that there's only one guy who can play Joey and that's Frank. He was *born* to play Joey. Why don't we give it a try?'

'OK, ask him,' said Cohn wearily.

Sidney put the idea to Sinatra the very next day. Sinatra said 'yes' before he had finished the question. He even said he'd buy into the project with his own independent company, Essex Productions.

Next came the casting, something that Cohn was adamant about. He was insistent that Rita Hayworth get top billing. He also demanded that Kim Novak be given the other lead role. How did Sinatra feel about that? He was now one of the world's most popular movie-stars. His name guaranteed success. He

109

had every right to kick up a fuss. 'Are you kidding?' he said when Sidney brought up the subject. 'Rita *is* Columbia Pictures. She has been ever since she stepped foot on the lot. Besides, who wouldn't agree to being in a sandwich between those two chicks,' he added with a twinkle in his eye.

Sinatra revelled in recreating Joey for the screen. He brought precisely the right amount of brashness and arrogance to the role and at the same time, through his own personality, softened Joey just enough to make him acceptable to movie audiences. He was still unscrupulous, still a climber, still a heel but a *likeable* heel.

Sinatra revelled too in the songs. Cohn had been ruthless with the original score. He had cut eight of the twelve original *Pal Joey* numbers and substituted in their stead such vintage Rodgers and Hart hits as 'I Didn't Know What Time It Was', 'There's a Small Hotel', 'My funny valentine' and 'What do I care for a dame?' It might not have been the original *Pal Joey* but it was a feast for Sinatra.

The stand-out number was suggested by George Sidney. It had featured in the 1937 Broadway hit *Babes In Arms* when it had been sung by Mitzi Green. The song was 'The Lady is a Tramp'. 'That's a woman's song,' scoffed Cohn. 'Sinatra will never sing that.'

'He'll go for it,' said Sidney, confidently. 'I'll talk with him.' But when he did bring it up during the pre-production planning of the movie the response was not what he had expected. Sinatra's reaction was cool. He showed no enthusiasm whatsoever. Sidney was forced to assume that on this occasion Cohn was right. He put the song aside as a non-starter.

Then came the call. Sinatra had just finished *The Joker Is Wild* and was in Vegas at the Sands. Sidney said:

> I got this telephone call. It was Frank. He said, 'Why don't you come up George, I've got a little something for you. Sinatra was doing two shows a night then (can you imagine what that would cost today?) and in those days he would sing ten numbers straight, one after the other and practically never stop, even for applause. I'd dropped in to see him in his dressing-room before the show and asked him what it was he wanted but he said, 'Later George, go out front and have some dinner and catch the show'.
>
> Well, he was well into his set numbers when right out of the

blue came 'Lady is a tramp'. I wasn't expecting it, nor was anyone else for that matter and he just tore the place apart. I'd never heard such a response to a song. Later, he came out and with a broad grin said, 'How do you like my new song?' That was Frank!

The changes to the original *Pal Joey* extended far beyond reworking the score otherwise Cohn would still have been unable to get the musical on the screen. Things had changed by 1957 but they hadn't changed that much. The married woman (now played by Rita Hayworth) was recast as a widow, the dialogue was toned down, and the locale changed from a seedy Chicago to a brighter, sunnier San Francisco. There was even a happy ending with Sinatra and Novak heading towards the Frisco Bridge and a rainbowed future. Most of the changes were acceptable enough considering the decision to soften the piece in the first place. The ending though was one step too far. 'I don't believe there were too many in the audience who swallowed all that,' recalled Sidney. 'I think they thought as I did. That the minute the bum got across the bridge he'd be off.'

What Columbia eventually came up with with *Pal Joey* was a bright, witty Technicolor musical that was 50 per cent Columbia and Harry Cohn and 50 per cent Rodgers and Hart and John O'Hara. For many it was a disappointment, a glossy toning down of a great musical. But for those who could accept the compromise and had never seen the original, which was most of the film's audience, and wanted to see Sinatra at the top of his form, it was a treat. Indeed so exhilarating was his rendering of the Rodgers and Hart numbers that it was almost as good as enjoying his act from a dinner table at the Sands.

Yet even with all the changes and the toning down there were still problems.

George Sidney explained:

I'd never had any problems with censorship in my life. But all of a sudden we heard there were problems with the film in New York. So I went to New York to find out what the trouble was all about.

There was a thing they ran in those days called 'The Legion of Decency' and a whole bunch of women had been complaining. Anyway, we ran the film and when it was over the women came over to me and said, 'It's the story of a pimp.'

I said, 'Really? Please give me a dictionary and tell me what a pimp is?' Well, a pimp was far from what Pal Joey was so that knocked that one down.

Then they said, 'Sinatra was a married man.'

(He was still married to Ava then) and I said, 'Where does Frank Sinatra appear up on the screen?' I said it's a *character*. 'Do you want to get into *my* personal life. What about the cameraman. He's been married six times you know. All this is ridiculous.'

Well, in the end they had nothing to say about it. There were no cuts, nothing. I couldn't believe the people I was dealing with. They were so far round Robin Hood's barn … as for Joey being a pimp. A pimp is a fellow who'll go up and down Sunset Boulevard. We have charming scenery here these days. And you know, he'll make a deal. That's *pimping*. It's a very old business. I hear profitable.'

When he viewed the finished film at Columbia Studios on Gower Street, Harry Cohn knew he was a lucky son-of-a-bitch. He had the last laugh on Hollywood after all. He usually did, he was a canny devil and had an instinctive feel for what the public wanted but there had been more than one occasion since he had purchased the rights to *Pal Joey* when he felt that, just for a change, Hollywood might have the last laugh on him. It didn't happen. As *Pal Joey* unspooled on screen before him he knew he had a great popular musical on his hands. Sinatra was sensational; 'Lady is a Tramp' was a knockout; Rita looked great; the orchestrations were superb. The whole film entertained. There was a song every ten minutes, sometimes there were two in that time. What gratified him most was that the film *moved*.

When someone reminded him that they were also releasing another prestigious film that fall – David Lean's classic war film *The Bridge On The River Kwai* – he shook his head. 'Great film, could win us a lot of Oscars. But it's 163 minutes. That's too long. Two hours is the maximum for a Columbia movie. *Pal Joey* is Columbia's film of the year.'

He told Sidney that he wanted a big preview for the picture, one of the biggest Columbia had ever staged. 'OK Harry,' said Sidney. 'We'll go to New York and show 'em what we've got. We'll book a theatre for the night and invite everybody, all the

people from Broadway.'
Sidney remembered later:

> It really was one helluva night. I spent the entire evening in the
> meat box. That's where you can control the sound and this, that
> and the other. I knew that unless it was done properly we were
> going to be killed. The Mermans, the Logans, everybody was
> there. We really had to do it in style. When we got to 'Lady is a
> Tramp' I just opened the box wide. I blew one of the speakers
> but there were six others so it was all right. Well, the audience
> they screamed, they cheered, they did everything ... it was so
> wonderful. Harry was over the moon.

Sinatra too was on a high. He had every reason to feel
satisfied with his interpretation of Joey Evans. His playing was
razor sharp. The gleam in his eye, the chip on his shoulder and
the charming insolence that weaved its way around every line of
dialogue and wisecrack brought Joey vividly to life.

For most of the critics it was a one-man show. In London's
Sunday Times, Dilys Powell, whilst regretting the absence of
the real *Pal Joey*, wrote:

> When at the showing the other afternoon we came to the point at
> which, for the benefit of the society woman visiting the third-rate
> night-club, he insolently sings 'that's why the lady is a tramp'
> there was a burst of applause from the audience and though
> these critical hands are not exactly horny with clapping I almost
> joined in.

Look Magazine added: 'Frank Sinatra plays Joey with all the
brass the role demands. He has a gleam in his eye and a chip on
his shoulder, as he portrays this unsavoury character who could
be so charming – against everybody's better judgment. He
tosses off both dames and songs with equal artistry.'

Variety too found him to be 'socko': 'Sinatra is potent. He's
almost ideal as the irreverent, free-wheeling, glib Joey,
delivering the rapid-fire cracks in a fashion that wrings out the
full deeper-than-pale-blue comedy potentials.' The *Hollywood
Reporter* summed him up thus:

> Sinatra does not cheat at all in his characterization. His Joey is as
> glittering and vulgar as a three carat little finger ring and still –
> and here is O'Hara's contribution – you are utterly fascinated

with his nasty little heel. You pull for his come-uppance but still, when he gets that kick in the teeth, you hope it does not disarrange them too much.

Audiences paid out nearly five million dollars to watch Sinatra and Hayworth and Novak in *Pal Joey*. It was one of Columbia's biggest ever musical successes. It was also one of the last enjoyed by Harry Cohn. In February 1958, just a few months after the première of *Pal Joey*, the film that had caused him trouble for almost fifteen years, he succumbed to cancer. He had been a bully for most of his working life yet for much of the time he had needed to be. Without him, Columbia studios would not have survived beyond the silent days of the twenties. In the thirties it had been the Capra comedies *and* Harry Cohn that had kept Columbia afloat; in the forties it had been Rita Hayworth and Harry Cohn; in the fifties, Harry Cohn's last decade, it had been a variety of things but Sinatra had more than played his part with his roles in *From Here To Eternity* and *Pal Joey*. Like George Sidney he was sad to see him go. There was no-one to enjoy fighting with anymore. When Cohn went so did a large part of the old Hollywood.

George Sidney still rates *Pal Joey* as his best screen musical – superior to anything he accomplished at MGM. He said later that he would like to have remade it as the *real Pal Joey* with Tom Jones, Sophia Loren and Mia Farrow and set it on the Riviera with all the rich girls and the yachts. But the opportunity never arose and in any case the memory of Sinatra's powerhouse delivery of 'Lady is a Tramp' was more than enough to keep him content.

Strangely, his most lasting memory of the film has nothing to do with what went on before or behind the cameras or what eventually finished up on screen. It has to do with what happened when he and Sinatra were chatting about nothing in particular outside Columbia Studios on Gower Street. He said

I can't remember exactly why we were there. The picture was finished I know that, it might have been some dubbing ... anyhow, we were standing there and a fella came by, somebody who had really been somebody, and we talked with him for a few minutes and then he went on his way, walking very slowly. It was terribly sad, an awful moment. I remember Frank watched him

114

for a long, long time. He didn't say anything until this man had turned the corner. Then he turned to me and said, 'You know George, nobody's ever going to say, "That used to be Frank Sinatra." ' And with that he got in his car and left. I've always remembered that moment. I guess Frank got his wish.

16   One-Take Charlie

'If directors keep him busy he maintains
an uneasy truce. Having started something, Sinatra's aim is to finish it – but
fast.'

Frank Capra

Sinatra's notorious impatience on set frequently brought
anxiety, even fear to his fellow performers. If they were slow
starters and needed time to warm to a scene it was often best to
bypass a Sinatra film altogether. If, on the other hand, they were
as sharp as he was, there could be a lot of pleasure from working
with 'Ol Blue Eyes'. The 'let's get at it' approach was
stimulating. It brought a charge and freshness to scenes.

Doris Day certainly found it invigorating. She liked the
spontaneity of early takes, as did Bing. And Bob Mitchum never
had any worries about keeping up with Frank. He knew it meant
he would always get home early. Mostly though, the stress of
getting things right on take one or take two brought problems.
Sinatra earned many nicknames because of his approach. Few
of them were complimentary. The one that stuck was 'One-
Take Charlie'.

Stars and directors had their own views as to why he felt the
need for speed. Gene Kelly believed it was the only way he
could get through a scene and feel he'd given of his best. During
the filming of *Pal Joey*, George Sidney opined:

Frank knows he's good. Whether it's in a movie or on a stage he
lets go ... it's like rehearsing. When you're blowing a trumpet
and you know the conductor's going to keep on rehearsing you're

116

not going to hit that high C. You're gonna lay off. But if this is the money, away you go. With Frank it was always, go, go, go …

Shirley MacLaine came up with the most ingenious theory. She felt that if Sinatra demonstrated that he'd been working hard on a movie and the movie didn't come off, he could offer no excuses. It was all down to him. If, on the other hand, he wasn't fully stretched, he could cover himself by replying that he wasn't really working up to his peak. People would then say to themselves: 'My goodness, think of what that man *could* do if he really worked.' Said MacLaine: 'Maybe he's afraid to see what might happen if he worked up to his full potential. It might destroy everything he'd done by playing it casual.'

In the late fifties many Hollywood directors found themselves coming face to face with the 'one-take' problem. Some accommodated Sinatra's technique without any trouble. Delmer Daves, for instance, got along with his star perfectly well on the war drama *Kings Go Forth*. So too did John Sturges on another war movie *Never So Few*. Even Vincente Minnelli, a perfectionist in his own right, enjoyed the challenges on *Some Came Running*. It was Frank Capra who experienced the greatest difficulties when he took on a film called *A Hole In The Head*. The picture was about a widower-cum-small-time promoter who is struggling to hold on to his 11-year-old son and the tatty, fleabag hotel he owns in Miami. It was hardly world-beating material but it marked Capra's first film in eight years so in that sense it was of some significance.

From Capra's point of view it was ideal, a lightweight co-production between Sinatra's independent company and his own. Sinatra was flying high at the box-office. What better way to get back into the mainstream.

Sinatra's first words when they met to set up the picture were, 'Cheech, why don't you and I make *A Hole In The Head* together. You do all the dirty work while I smile and knock off all the broads.' To Capra it seemed a reasonable attitude. This is going to be a breeze, he thought. He was wrong.

The first day of shooting brought him face to face with the problem. He knew that Sinatra liked to work fast. He had expected that. What he hadn't anticipated was that if things didn't quite go as planned Sinatra's performance would lose its freshness. He was great on take one – couldn't be better. He was everything a director could ask for. By take two he'd lost something. The edge had gone. What is more it had gone for good. By take three he was faltering and beyond three, he was lost.

Capra groaned. Not again, he thought. Not *twice* in one's career. Just what have I done to deserve this? His mind went back almost thirty years to a Columbia picture he'd made called *Ladies Of Leisure*. The star of the film had been Barbara Stanwyck. Always, without exception, she had been word perfect on the first take. It didn't matter whether she was being photographed in close-up, in long shot or whether she was just rehearsing. *Always*, it was exactly right. But when her co-stars stumbled and needed more time she got progressively worse. After half-a-dozen shouts of 'action!' from Capra she was but a pale copy of the Stanwyck who had given her all on take one.

Capra had got round the problem by discussing things with Stanwyck on her own in her dressing room. He had explained the meaning of the scene, the points that should be brought out, the nuances, the pauses and so on. That way he knew she would arrive on set and never blow a line. Always, his last instruction to her was, 'Remember Barbara. No matter what the other actors do, whether they stop or stumble over their words, you continue your scene right to the end. Understand? Good girl.'

And that's the way he got through it – one camera focusing solely on Stanwyck, one on the other actors in the scene, and a third covering everyone. If things went wrong and the other actors needed retakes he knew he had Stanwyck in the can. Later, he could mesh everything together in the cutting room. The technique worked every time in the five movies they made together.

It quickly became apparent, however, that it wouldn't work with Sinatra. He may have been Stanwyck mark two but the idea of sitting alone in his dressing room and discussing things with Capra was anathema to him. He liked to be part of the whole set-up. He liked the buzz. It got his adrenalin going.

Capra decided on a different line of approach – improvisation. That way, he reasoned, only the feelings of the screenwriter would get hurt. It didn't take long for him to bring the approach into play.

118

The scene being filmed was at a Miami dog track. It required Sinatra to try and touch an old pal, played by Keenan Wynn, for some urgently needed cash. No dice. Sinatra finishes up humiliated. And also in pain as he throws fifty bucks in Wynn's face and gets a right hook in the solar plexus in return.

Capra sensed from the outset that things would be difficult. The scene wasn't complicated but it was busy. Several people were involved, there was a bit of action and the timing of the dialogue had to be exactly right. With misgivings Capra called for the first rehearsal. As usual, Sinatra was great. It was the others who needed straightening out. The second rehearsal and this time Sinatra was not so good and starting to cool off. The others though had improved. The first photographic take and Sinatra was stone cold. The others were fine.

The atmosphere on set darkened. The technicians sensed a tension that had not been there half-an-hour before.

'OK, one more time Frank,' called Capra.

Sinatra, sullen and indifferent, his mouth now hardened into a tough line, seemed reluctant to give it another try.

'Something bothering you Frank?'

Sinatra spat it out, 'Hell, yes, all these rehearsals and repeating the same jokes to the same jerks. It'd bother *anybody*!'

'OK, Frank, we'll sort it out.'

Capra went into a huddle with the other actors. Forget the script, he told them. Make up your own lines, mix things up a little bit, make it different. To Keenan Wynn he said, 'Change your cues, say different lines of dialogue, make sure Frank doesn't know what's coming next. Surprise him.'

It was the perfect ploy. Sinatra reacted as though he were in a completely new scene. The spark was there, the enthusiasm was back. Capra even arranged for the position of the extras to be changed. Anything to give the scene a new look. The end result was a wonderful sequence, full of natural ad-libs.

Later, when he met up with Billy Wilder at a meeting of the Director's Guild, Capra mentioned the success he'd had in directing Sinatra and how well things had worked out. Wilder had been a close friend of Sinatra's for many years. He expressed the view that Capra had been lucky. Several times he'd refused point blank to work with the actor. Said Wilder, 'I'm afraid he would run after the first take. Bye, bye kid, that's it. I'm going. I've got to see a chick. That would drive me crazy. 'Besides,' he added with a wry smile, 'you wouldn't find me offering him the chance to change any of *my* scripts.'

There was one occasion, however, when Wilder did actually get within a whisker of working with Sinatra, and in the very same year as Capra was shooting *A Hole In The Head*. Wilder was having trouble getting finance for his classic drag comedy *Some Like It Hot*. United Artists were dubious. 'Who wants to see a movie about two jazz musicians dressed as girls?'

'I do,' said Wilder.

Blank response. United Artists thought it might be a starter if Wilder could get someone other than Jack Lemmon. Tony Curtis was OK but Lemmon was still finding his feet. How about Sinatra? Wilder was reluctant. All those chicks! He decided to give it a try. He arranged a meeting to see how Sinatra felt about things. The meeting was set for Vegas. Sinatra never showed. Lemmon got the role which was what Wilder had wanted all along.

The end result couldn't have been bettered, Lemmon was a nigh on perfect 'Daphne' but the prospect of Sinatra, Monroe and Curtis working together from a Wilder/Diamond script remains one of the most mouthwatering of all cinematic 'might-have-beens'.

A Hole In The Head turned out to be a box-office smash. Sinatra and his co-stars, Edward G. Robinson, Eleanor Parker and Thelma Ritter all received good notices and Sinatra sang his third Oscar winning song in just six years – the bouncy 'High Hopes' which he performed with the young Eddie Hodges. The box-office take of the film was a healthy $4,000,000.

Capra would dearly have liked to have worked with Sinatra again and two years later felt he had the perfect role, that of Dave The Dude in *Pocketful Of Miracles*, a remake of his pre-war hit *Lady For A Day*. It was based on a Damon Runyon tale and would have suited Sinatra rather more than his previous foray into Runyon territory some six years earlier. The film, however, could not be slotted into Sinatra's schedule and Capra had to settle instead for Glenn Ford, as far as he was concerned a far from adequate replacement.

In the end, it was perhaps for the best. As Capra later reflected, Sinatra was a fine screen performer but given the chance he would always settle for being where the action was and that was not a film set. For him the somewhat lukewarm reactions of cameramen, script girls and dead-pan technicians, busy, dispassionate people who had seen it all before, were somewhat less attractive than the enthusiasms of his fellow performers and those Capra referred to as 'the lovelies'. Said Capra: 'The film set is torture for him. There's no audience. He is not Sinatra doing Sinatra's thing with a song. He can't bewitch like he can with a live, ever-changing saloon audience.'

For all the criticisms levelled at him about his desire to get things done in double quick time before the cameras Sinatra was not impervious to the frustrations of his fellow actors. Time and again he went out of his way to stress that he was not a crammer. He was not an actor who read his lines the night before, came on set, said them and then left. That was not his style. On a major film he would read the entire script as many as fifty times, taking it with him wherever he went – to his office, the bedroom, keeping it by the telephone, even in the john. When it came to a particular scene he would simply glance at the script to remember the lines and just how the scene fitted into the picture as a whole.

Always he would attempt to understand the motivations and reactions of the man he was playing and how he fitted into the overall story. Always he would listen carefully to the lines of his fellow actors. And for good reason. Over the years he had discovered that co-stars were quick to steal whatever they could from a scene and did so without batting an eyelid. Spencer Tracy, for instance. He was sharper than any other actor in the business. Said Sinatra: 'With Spence you don't have time between his lines and yours to think about what you have to say next.'

Sinatra played opposite Tracy just the once – in a 1962 movie called *The Devil At Four O'Clock*, made by veteran Mervyn LeRoy. It was about three convicts who helped some children escape from a volcanic island. Tracy played an ageing priest, Sinatra one of the convicts. It wasn't a good picture but it was an interesting star combination. Tracy was an MGM veteran of the 'I go to my marks and say my lines 'philosophy. He, too, liked to get it on take one. It was one of the very few movies in which Sinatra received as good as he gave. Not surprisingly, his admiration for Tracy knew no bounds.

17   The Film That Never Was

'A note to Sinatra ... you are not giving
employment to a poor little sheep who
has lost his way but are making available
a story wide open for the communist
line.'

Los Angeles Examiner

In 1960 Sinatra threw in his lot with John F. Kennedy, the
young senator from Massachusetts, who was seeking the
Democratic presidential nomination.

The two men had known each other since the days when
Kennedy had frequented Hollywood sets to secretly romance
the beautiful Gene Tierney. The relationship had blossomed
through Sinatra's long-standing friendship with Kennedy's
brother-in-law, actor Peter Lawford. In the late fifties it had
become even closer when Kennedy was frequently glimpsed in
Las Vegas where Sinatra and his buddies, soon to become
known as The Clan, knocked 'em dead each night in cabaret at
the Sands Hotel.

The friendship between the two men spelt danger to the
Republicans. The word was that whoever won the upcoming
political battle, which it was assumed would be between
Kennedy and Nixon, the result would be close. Nixon had been
Eisenhower's vice-president for eight years. As the man who
had held public office he was deemed to have the advantage. He
had also received Eisenhower's public endorsement.

Kennedy was the challenger. He was young, good-looking
and charming. He was also a Catholic and a Catholic had never
before held presidential office. He faced prejudice and smear all

the way along the line. If the result was to be as close as the pundits were predicting he needed every vote he could get. Sinatra, he knew, would he helpful in securing the Italian-American vote. His campaigning could be crucial. But first he needed the nomination. Sinatra's song 'High Hopes' was adopted as the campaign song and the bandwagon began to roll.

An anxious right wing needed something to tarnish the image of the two golden boys. Kennedy and Sinatra was a potentially lethal combination. Ironically, it was Sinatra himself who gave them the ammunition they needed.

In March of 1960 he announced that his next film project would be William Bradford Huie's *The Execution Of Private Slovik*, the true story of the only American soldier to be executed for desertion since the Civil War. Huie was a former newspaper man who had authored many books about racism and human rights. He had spent years delving into the archives to find out the precise facts about the man who had gone before a military firing squad in 1945. His was a controversial book and Sinatra hoped it would make an equally controversial film. The picture would be Sinatra's own personal project. He would produce and possibly direct. He would not appear.

The announcement raised a few eyebrows but nothing more. A provocative picture, yes, but there were other movies in production that looked just as interesting. Besides, the book had been in print since 1954. It wasn't exactly hot off the press.

The bombshell came when Sinatra announced his choice of screenwriter. Albert Maltz, he said, would pen the script. Right-wingers immediately sat up and took notice.

Maltz had last received credit for *The Naked City* in 1948. Two years later he had been indicted, along with nine other writers and directors, for contempt of Congress. As one of the 'Hollywood Ten' he had declined to answer questions put by the House Un-American Activities Committee regarding his membership of the Communist Party. He had also refused to name names and inform on other colleagues with left-wing sympathies. The result was a $1,000 fine and a year in prison. Blacklisted by the Hollywood studios he moved to Mexico where, like Dalton Trumbo and others, he sold screenplays and his services under a pseudonym. His drop in earnings was considerable. From $3,000 a week to $2,500 a script. A

123

celebrated author in his own right, he earned a living by writing short stories and novels.

Sinatra's decision to employ Maltz turned out to be a terrible miscalculation. A natural Democrat and a man who detested the blacklist and all its implications, he believed he was following a trend. In his eyes the blacklist had already been broken earlier in the year when Otto Preminger had announced that Dalton Trumbo would be writing the screenplay of his next epic, *Exodus* and that he would be receiving full credit. Producer/star Kirk Douglas followed suit by stating that Trumbo would also be receiving credit for his work on *Spartacus*. A third film-maker Stanley Kramer also went public by acknowledging that one of the writers on his *Inherit The Wind* was the blacklisted Nedrich Young. Sinatra reasoned with some justification: if Trumbo and Young, why not Maltz?

Things, however, were a little more complicated than that. As he very quickly discovered Sinatra had badly misread the situation. Preminger was a film-maker and nothing more. He could do what he liked. So could Kirk Douglas and Stanley Kramer. All had firm political convictions but none was openly campaigning for Kennedy – Sinatra was. He had one of the highest profiles of the Kennedy campaign. What he said or did could affect votes. The Republican press pounced. Mike Connolly in the *Hollywood Reporter* was one of the first to dig in the knife. He wrote, 'Sinatra is a commie apologist and Maltz is a "sneaky, switch-hunting, strikebreaking fink".' The *Los Angeles Examiner* joined in the condemnation, 'A note to Sinatra … you are not giving employment to a poor little sheep who has lost his way but are making available a story wide open for the communist line. Therefore we suggest you consider thoughtfully the request of National Commander Raymond O'Leary of the Catholic War Veterans. Dump Maltz and get yourself a true American.'

For their part, the Hearst Newspapers suggested that 'The impact of Mr Sinatra's move may cause dismay in the campaign camp of Senator John F. Kennedy.'

Sensing that the momentum of the story was building nicely against Sinatra, and also indirectly against Kennedy, John Wayne chipped in with his strident views. He was then actively involved in making his tribute to Americanism, *The Alamo. He* was the true American. Sinatra was not. The public, he knew, would side with him. They considered him a war hero even though he had never worn a uniform other than that provided by a Hollywood wardrobe department.

Wayne went for the kill. He said publicly, 'I wonder how Sinatra's crony John Kennedy feels about him hiring such a man. I'd like to know his attitude because he's the one who is making plans to run the administrative government of our country.'

Sinatra hit back. He had never been a quitter. If he believed in a cause he fought hard and long. He took heart from an editorial in the *New York Post* that applauded him for taking his stand, 'An Oscar to Frank. He has joined the select company of Hollywood valiants who have declared their independence from the Un-American Activities Committee and the American Legion in defying the secret blacklist.' Frank put his case by taking out a full page in the Hollywood trade papers:

> This type of partisan politics is hitting below the belt. I spoke to many screenwriters but it was not until I talked to Albert Maltz that I found a writer who saw the screenplay in exactly the terms I wanted. This is, the army was right. Under our bill of rights I was taught that no one may prescribe what shall be orthodox in politics, religion or other matters of opinion.
>
> As producer and director of the film I and I alone will be responsible for it. I am concerned that the screenplay reflects the true pro-American values of the story. I am prepared to stand on my principles and to wait the verdict of the American people when they see *The Execution Of Private Slovik*. I repeat, in my role as a picture-maker I have in my opinion, hired the best man to do the job.

It was brave, fighting stuff – but it was defensive stuff. Sinatra's back was to the wall and he knew it. Noises were beginning to come from the Kennedy camp. The right-wing press stepped up a gear. Hedda Hopper, a gossip columnist heard and read by millions, opined, 'If Sinatra loves his country he won't do this. He'll write off the cost of the story and forget it. But will he? He's stubborn. But he's not viciously pig headed. He has a fine family of which he is proud. Will he do it for them?'

That Sinatra would be the eventual loser in the affair became apparent when priests began to sermonize against him in their pulpits. Alarm bells began to ring in Democratic headquarters. Ambassador Kennedy called Cardinal Spellman in New York and Cardinal Cushing in Boston. How serious was this Hollywood business? Very serious. Sinatra was seen consorting with communists. It could only damage his son's campaign for the presidency.

When a governor in New Hampshire accused Kennedy of being soft on communism, Joe Kennedy moved swiftly. He called Sinatra and arranged an urgent meeting. At the meeting it boiled down to one simple sentence, 'Frank, it's either Maltz or us.'

Friends and fellow actors who had known Sinatra for years still believed he would hold fast. Robert Mitchum said, 'The only man in town I'd be afraid to fight is Frank Sinatra. I might knock him down but he'd keep getting up until one of us was dead.'

On 1 April, however, it was Sinatra who was the corpse. He issued a statement from his home in Palm Springs:

> Due to the reactions of my family, my friends and the American public, I have instructed my attorneys to make a settlement with Albert Maltz and to inform him that he will not write the screenplay of *The Execution Of Private Slovik*. I had thought the major consideration was whether or not the resulting script would be in the best interests of the United States. Since my conversation with Mr Maltz had indicated that he had an affirmative pro-American approach to the story and since I felt fully capable as producer of enforcing such standards, I have defended my hiring of Mr Maltz. But the American public has indicated that it feels the morality of hiring Mr Maltz is the more crucial matter and I will accept the majority opinion.

The *Los Angeles Examiner* gloated in triumph. It ran an eight column streamer in red above its own masthead, SINATRA OUSTS MALTZ AS WRITER!

Chastened, Sinatra paid Maltz the full $75,000 he had promised him for the script. He was too embarrassed to call Maltz and apologize.

For his part, Maltz took the money, returned to Mexico and carried on writing. He did eventually receive another screen credit – in 1970 for his work on Don Siegel's *Two Mules For Sister Sara*. He made no comment about the affair other than to remark in later years that he had been surprised that Sinatra had made the announcement when he did. It might have been better to write the script first, get the film made and then announce the author when the film was ready for release – like Preminger had done with *Exodus*. Said Maltz:

> Frank told me it was very important for him to make the film. He said that if anyone tried to interfere with his hiring me they were going to run into a buzz saw. He anticipated all the problems and the outcry from the American Legion types but he said he didn't care and wanted to break the blacklist. I just don't think he took account of the political consequences that's all.

The liberal press were mainly sympathetic towards Sinatra for reversing his decision. Not too many people had been forced to take on the right-wing, veteran groups, the newspapers and the Church all in one go. The miracle was that he had lasted out as long as he had.

The only hint of rage from Sinatra came when he came face to face with John Wayne at The Moulin Rouge nightclub in Hollywood in May. The occasion was a charity dinner. Wayne said a friendly 'hello'. Witnesses said that Sinatra immediately began berating him for publicly opposing the hiring of Maltz. There were belligerent stares but no fisticuffs. Another version has it that the pair came across each other in the carpark. Frank had been drinking. 'You seem to disagree with me,' he snarled at the 6 ft. 4 in. actor.

'Not now, Frank, some other time,' said Wayne walking away. Friends had to hold Sinatra back.

The end result was that Sinatra carefully avoided all publicity until the Democratic convention in July. The time between the Maltz announcement and the Maltz withdrawal was eighteen days. *The Execution Of Private Slovik* was dropped by Sinatra.

It did eventually get made, in 1974 as a two-and-a-half hour TV movie at Universal. Maltz did not write the script. Richard Levinson and William Link were responsible for the writing. Sinatra had no hand in the production. Martin Sheen played Eddie Slovik and earned an Emmy nomination for his portrayal.

Ten years later he earned more acclaim for another TV portrayal – as John F. Kennedy.

Perhaps, in the end, Sinatra did make the right decision even though it was painful at the time. Otto Preminger later revealed that before employing Trumbo to write his screenplay for *Exodus* he had first approached Leon Uris the author of the novel on which the film was based. When that didn't work out he sought the services of the blacklisted Maltz who was living in Mexico. 'I tried to finish the script with Maltz,' said Otto. 'He was very impressive to watch. Whenever I visited him I found him surrounded by tables piled high with research material he was collecting. But he never got round to writing a line.'

Back at the piano and back at Metro! Off-set with Debbie Reynolds
during the filming of *The Tender Trap*

A couple of high-rollers! Sinatra as Nathan Detroit and Marlon Brando as Sky Masterson in Sam Goldwyn's film version of the musical *Guys And Dolls*

Close to his best! Sinatra as singer-turned night-club entertainer Joe E. Lewis in *The Joker Is Wild*

Sinatra meets Rodgers and Hart – and a dog – in George Sidney's glossy version of *Pal Joey*

In pensive mood. Sharing thoughts with director Frank Capra during the filming of *A Hole In The Head*

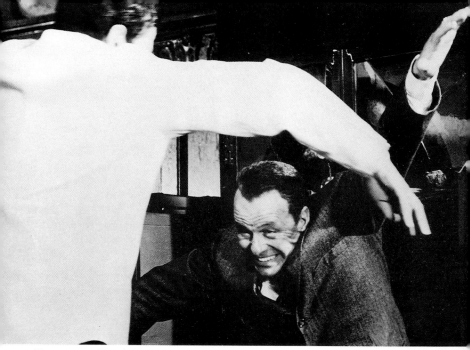

East meets West! Sinatra hots up the Cold War in *The Manchurian Candidate*

Reliving the nightmares of brainwashing. Sinatra and Laurence Harvey in *The Manchurian Candidate*

Three members of the Clan in *Robin And The Seven Hoods. Left to right:*
Dean Martin, Sammy Davis, jun. and Sinatra

Comedy can be a serious business! Sinatra rehearsing with Lee J. Cobb
(right) on the set of *Come Blow Your Horn*

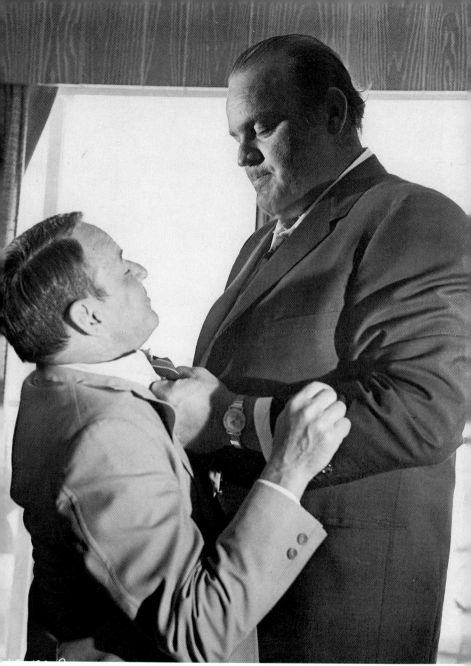

No contest! Sinatra up against ex-convict Dan Blocker in the private-eye thriller *Lady In Cement*

Sinatra in the opening sequence of *The Detective* and coming face to face with the mutilated corpse of a murdered homosexual

Same film, different problem. Sinatra's Detective Joe Leland trying to come to terms with estranged wife Lee Remick

18   The Manchurian Candidate

'It was the only film I know that went from failure to classic without passing through success.'

George Axelrod

It was director John Frankenheimer and screenwriter George Axelrod who brought the book to Sinatra's attention. They were downhearted. No one thought it would make a good movie. They did. Did he? The book was *The Manchurian Candidate*.

The book fascinated Sinatra. He couldn't make up his mind whether it was a satire of the right-wing or the left-wing. Or whether it was an indictment of the red-baiters of the fifties or a scathing attack on communism. Or, indeed, whether it was any of these things. The tone was quirky, the mood sombre one minute, bizarre and irreverent the next. It was the first film since *Private Slovik* that had really interested him.

He put the idea up to Arthur Krim who was president of United Artists. Normally, it was just the kind of thing Krim would have gone for – a fast-moving conspiracy thriller that was different and controversial. He was surprised when Krim gave it the thumbs down. When he enquired as to the reason, Krim, who was a big wheel in the Democratic Party, told him that he thought the film was too sensitive. It was also, in his view, anti-communist. John Kennedy was about to attempt a peace initiative with the Russians. To release a picture that showed the commies up to some very dirty tricks was not exactly what was

129

required at that precise moment. Sinatra protested that he was over-reacting. It was only a movie after all, a piece of make-believe. Besides, in his view, the film was not anti-communist. The way he read it, it was anti-everything. Krim would have none of it. He vetoed *The Manchurian Candidate*.

Sinatra's relationship with Kennedy had cooled in the aftermath of the Presidential victory, primarily because it was deemed unseemly for Kennedy to be seen in the company of a man who still enjoyed the boisterous company of such Rat Pack buddies as Dean Martin, Sammy Davis and Joey Bishop. The two men though were still friendly enough for Sinatra to bypass Krim and appeal directly to the President about the filming of *The Manchurian Candidate*. Kennedy loved the book. Richard Condon was one of his favourite authors. He agreed with Sinatra. It would make a great movie. Sinatra mentioned that Krim thought it too dangerous. Kennedy smoothed his fears. He would have a word. He told Sinatra to go ahead. As a last thought, he asked, 'Who the hell are you going to get to play the mother?'

It was a good question. To cast someone as a woman who had been described by one critic as 'what Lady Macbeth would have been like if she'd been a mother' was one of the main problems facing Frankenheimer and Sinatra when they came to cast the movie which kept close to Condon's original, and was enlivened still further by Axelrod's translation of some of Condon's descriptive passages into witty and lively dialogue.

The complex story revolved around the fiendish brainwashing and hypnosis of a group of American soldiers who are captured in Korea and then returned to the States unaware that one of them is primed to carry out a political assassination at a pre-arranged command. The assassination is due to take place at a rally at Madison Square Garden. Once it has occurred, the parents of the assassin – one a red-baiting McCarthy senator (in reality a Moscow plant), the other his wife, would finish up in the White House. Bizarre, highly improbable, but hugely enjoyable.

Laurence Harvey was named for the role of the assassin, Sinatra as one of his brainwashed buddies who helps track him down and Janet Leigh was slipped in to deliver some weird and erotic wisecracks (similar to those exchanged between Bogart and Bacall in *The Big Sleep*) to lighten things when the occasion demanded. For the killer's mother, a dominating ogress of a woman who is the brains behind the whole operation, they chose the powerfully erotic Angela Lansbury. 'Great,' said Kennedy when he heard the news. 'She'll be perfect!'

Frankenheimer was a fast director. Like many of his contemporaries he'd come from television. He completed the film in thirty-nine days, four of which were devoted to the assassination attempt in Madison Square Garden. Other scenes were shot in a local California Stadium called the Olympic Auditorium and on sound stages in Hollywood.

After viewing the film at a private screening Sinatra said, 'It is, without doubt, the finest picture I have ever made. The trouble is I don't know what to say when people ask me what it's about other than to tell them that every night, while making the picture, I stayed up worrying about the part.'

Sinatra pulled his weight throughout the making of the film – except once. That was only a minor skirmish. It occurred when Frankenheimer wasn't happy with a take and wanted to go again. It was late in the day. Frankenheimer decided to wait until morning and refilm the scene then. Nothing annoyed Sinatra more than having to wait overnight to reshoot a scene he thought had gone well in the first place.

George Axelrod remembered:

He'd been on time every day but he wasn't there the next morning. We waited and waited and about two o'clock in the afternoon you could feel this black cloud coming up Santa Monica Boulevard and turning down Formosa.

Sinatra marched in, went straight to his dressing-room and slammed the door without a word. An hour later he appeared on set, in costume, full of rage. Larry Harvey looked at him and said, 'Oh, my dear, we're having our period today are we?' The whole set broke up. Sinatra started to laugh and everything was fine from then on.

Without Sinatra *The Manchurian Candidate* would never have got made. Frankenheimer, Axelrod and Condon all accepted that. Had any other producer or studio tried to have got it off the ground they would have failed. 'Few stars carried that much clout in those days,' said Axelrod. 'We were equal partners except that Sinatra was more equal, as is his custom.'

Frankheimer was lucky to get the film at all. He had originally been slated for *Breakfast At Tiffany's* when Audrey Hepburn brought a halt to the proceedings with a 'Who's he?'. He was replaced by Blake Edwards. Edwards did a craftsmanlike job on *Tiffany's* but it is doubtful whether he could have equalled the flair that Frankenheimer brought to *The Manchurian Candidate*. The brainwashing sequence especially, is superb as the American prisoners, in reality being hypnotized by the Koreans, believe themselves to be at a ladies' garden party. The camera, constantly circling and all the time moving round and round the prisoners, brilliantly emphasizes the Americans' confused state of mind.

The press reaction to *The Manchurian Candidate* was mixed. The *New York Times* was one of those in favour of the film, 'As a puzzler and a dynamic thriller and even Freudian satire this one will glue you to your seat.' *Variety* too found much to praise highlighting the 'top performances, the literally stunning climax and the sheer bravado of narrative and photographic style'.

Others, however, found it incomprehensible. They were uncertain of what they were watching. In 1962 black comedy had not made very deep inroads into cinema entertainment. *Dr Strangelove* was still two years away. Were people supposed to laugh? Were they supposed to cry or were they supposed to be on the edge of their seats? The film's amoral stance, its high camp visuals and sly, sardonic humour was beyond them. Audiences too were baffled. The expected box-office success did not materialize. The film cost $3 million. It failed to make its money back. Frankenheimer blamed United Artists for not pushing it hard enough. He said later, 'They didn't know what they had and they didn't support the movie.' George Axelrod added wryly:

It was the only film I know that went from failure to classic without passing through success.

It was one of those things that was ahead of its time. You get pictures like that from time to time. Audiences found it incomprehensible and confusing. It was picketed on the Champs-Elysée in Paris by the Communist Party who said it was American fascist propaganda. On the same day it was picketed in Orange County in California by the American Legion who said it was Communist propaganda.

As far as Frankenheimer was concerned there was no problem with the film. For him it was about the political situation in the country at the time. He said:

> This counry was just recovering from the McCarthy era and nothing had ever been filmed about it. I wanted to do a picture that showed how ludicrous the whole McCarthy far right syndrome was and how dangerous the far left was. The film really dealt with the McCarthy era, the whole idea of fanaticism, the far right and the far left being exactly the same thing and the total idiocy of it. I wanted to show that and I think we did.

The one man who loved the film was President Kennedy. Sinatra arranged for him to receive his own special print, delivering it at the time of the film's release in November 1962. Kennedy sent a cable congratulating everyone on a wonderful job. A year later he was dead from an assassin's bullet. Those critics, and there were many, who had scoffed at the film for being too far fetched were silenced. Instead they turned on the film from a different viewpoint, deeming it to be in bad taste in the face of real political tragedy and the theories that followed in the wake of events in Dallas.

Sinatra was at work on one of his Clan movies, *Robin And The Seven Hoods* when news of the assassination came through. It signalled the end of Kennedy's Camelot and the end of the rat pack encampment outside its fairyland walls. The carefree days of high hopes and partying were over.

Sinatra was said to be so racked with guilt over the association between the movie and Kennedy's death that he had the picture withdrawn after the assassination. Angela Lansbury commented, 'Mr Sinatra felt that it was a dangerous picture to have around.'

Frankenheimer believed that there was a more simple explanation for the picture's disappearance. He felt that United Artists accountants had forced the film into a loss-making position by procedures he called 'questionable, to say the least'. It was this financial impasse said Frankheimer that prevented any re-release of the film.

Suggestions that the film was withdrawn were, in any case, mistaken. The film did play network television at least once in the States in the sixties and was only taken out of circulation in 1972 by Sinatra who had full contractual rights over its release.

Axelrod said, 'Frank didn't seem to be aware of the fact that he was holding it back. He had so many things going on that I'm sure he just forgot about it. When it was suggested that the film should be re-issued after a sell-out screening at the New York Film Festival, he agreed without hesitation.'

With its unique tone of paranoid satire *The Manchurian Candidate* stands as one of Sinatra's finest films. His performance as Bennett Marco is not one of his showiest roles. It is a quiet compelling characterization of some sensitivity. It is a solid portrayal. His sweat is the life blood of a movie that, even today, some thirty odd years after its first release, still serves as a chilling reminder that things are not always what they seem in the modern world. The *New Yorker* said of his performance, 'Sinatra, in his usual, uncanny fashion, is simply terrific.'

Sinatra made other pictures in the early sixties. In most of them – *Can-Can, Ocean's Eleven, Sergeants Three* – he appeared to be sleepwalking through his parts, perhaps because of his bitter experiences in trying to get *Private Slovik* off the ground. *The Manchurian Candidate* made up for all of them. It was American film-making at its best and it was Sinatra at his best. It was just a shame it didn't show a profit.

19   Hollywood and Sammy Cahn

'He said, "How would you like Gene Kelly *and* Saul Chaplin?"
I said, "Frank we're home and free." '
                                    Sammy Cahn

Another personal intrusion. This time the spinner of tales is songwriter Sammy Cahn. The place: his elegant residence in Beverly Hills. The time: early Saturday morning, just before breakfast. The interview room: Cahn's study, well laced with orange juice and coffee. I am ushered to the most comfortable seat in the room. Cahn plants himself in front of the myriad of photographs and framed certificates that line his walls. The purpose of the interview? To discuss his movie songs for a BBC radio series that will trace the history of the Hollywood musical.

An attractive, bronzed, dark-haired girl in her late teens jogs in bathed in Californian sweat. She grins a 'hi!' and sinks to the ground against a wall. There are no introductions. Cahn is worried. Should he take it off the hook? The telephone that is? Yes. No! Leave it, it's early. We'll get through.

We start. Astaire, Doris Day, Monroe are among the first stars we discuss but Sinatra is never far away. He seems to intrude on every other story. We reach the 1964 musical *Robin And The Seven Hoods*, the one in which Sinatra plays a kind of Sherwood outlaw of Chicago in the twenties.

A look of resignation, almost displeasure, crosses Cahn's face. The film is apparently not a favourite topic. I debate as to whether to move on but Cahn is under way and once under way it is difficult to stop him.

'It was a lot of fun to write but it could have been so much better,' he says. 'It could have been a triumph of a movie musical, if only it had had the right people and I thought it had at first.'

Cahn shakes his head at the memory. 'When Sinatra called me and said, "We got an idea for a great musical Sammy," I said, "What is this?" He said, "*Robin And The Seven Hoods*, the old Robin Hood story set in Chicago in the Prohibition days." '

'I said, "It's sensational" but I said, "However, I *beg* you, I *caution* you," cause he can be very wilful, he can be very very wilful, I said, "if you're going to go ahead with this get some pros – some of the former MGM guys who know how to put this sort of thing together. A producer like Saul Chaplin, Gene Kelly, people like that. Someone who will know how to take the printed page to the screen." '

'Anyway, he called me again and said, "Are you *ready*?" '

'I said, "I'm *ready*." '

'He said, "How would you like Gene Kelly *and* Saul Chaplin?" '

'I said, "Frank, we're home and free!" '

'But I was mistaken. I thought he meant Gene Kelly to direct and Saul Chaplin to produce. But it wasn't the case. He had Gordon Douglas to direct. Gene Kelly was going to produce and Saul Chaplin supervise the music. We weren't into the picture about three weeks when Gene Kelly stepped aside. There was some difference of opinion, I forget what it was. Two weeks later Saul Chaplin stepped aside taking a bit of my heart away with him.

'So what I had hoped would be one of the great, great glittering musicals became what is on the screen now.' He pulls a face and shrugs. 'The idea for the film was so good in itself that they couldn't defeat it totally but if they'd had the expertise of Kelly and Chaplin it would have been something else.'

I mention 'My Kind Of Town', one of the great Sinatra songs Cahn had written for the movie. Before Cahn can answer the phone rings. It isn't too early. He gets into an involved discussion about writing something for a benefit. Can he fit it in? He'll be in New York. When will he be back? He doesn't know.

The conversation gets complicated. The girl rises and pours us coffee. The conversation ends. 'Keep the phone off the hook for a while darling,' he says to the bronzed youngster. 'Where was I?'

' "My Kind Of Town",' I prompted.

'Oh yeah … well, I wish I could say it was hard to write but in all honesty it wasn't. What was unusual about the writing was that there was, of course, already a song about Chicago, a great song that had been around for years. Sinatra had sung it, everyone had sung it.

'Anyway, when they asked me to write this song I was obviously not going to write a song with Chicago in the title. So I said to Jimmy Van Heusen, "We'll go round through the back door." I said, "How about My kind of town, Chicago is my kind of town?" So one word leads to another and finally you've got it. And that's how we wrote the song. The fact that it was about Chicago was really incidental. It could have been about any town. I forget how long it took us. An hour maybe, perhaps two. That song was a hit almost from the beginning.'

He paused and waved an accusatory finger at no one in particular, 'You know the best song in that picture? "I Like To Lead When I Dance".'

I confess I don't know it.

'You wouldn't. It never appeared. When he heard it Sinatra felt it was the best Sinatra song he had ever heard. It's the song which sets the scene for the whole film, when Barbara Rush – she played a gangster's daughter in the movie – is coming on to Sinatra, acting as if she was Sinatra coming on to *her*.

'What I mean is, she's in the room with him, she's putting out all the lights, she's feeding him the booze and he looks at her all fish-eyed you know and sings, "But I'm the one who's going to lead, I'll set the speed. I've got to lead if we dance". And he was supposed to sing that song to her. Then, as the movie proceeds the song is reprised when she tries it on with Dean Martin and he sings it to her. When she tries to get Victor Buono, the same thing happens. Everytime she tries to get someone the song is reprised.

'Sinatra loved the song beyond loving a song. He'd recorded it for the film. The day of the shooting came. He was a little bit under the weather. Whatever the reason, he didn't do the song.

It was never in the film. One of the real crushing blows of my life. It was one of the best ... oh well.'

He laughs, stands and shows me to the door. The interview is over. A lot of telephone calls have been piling up. Probably requests for more songs for him to write. The record books say that he had written the lyrics for more than 2,500 movie-songs. Was that true I ask as I step out into the Los Angeles sunshine. 'They say it is,' says Sammy. 'I haven't got the time to count.'

He thanks me for coming. The bronzed girl has disappeared. 'You know something about Sinatra? He can move into a lyric like it was a house. Eighty-seven songs, that's how many I've written for him, eighty-seven and some of my best – "Three Coins", "All The Way", "The Tender Trap", "Time After Time" ... I just wish he'd done "I Like To Lead When I Dance". But that's Frank. He's a man of many moods, some of them dark.

'You put up with that of course. Otherwise, you get back into what Billy Wilder calls "normal".

'You know what he says, "If you want normal forget Sinatra or Monroe or Garland. Get your Uncle Irving. He'll turn up on time and be there next morning. And he'll do what he's told." ' Sammy laughs. 'But he won't be Sinatra, something will be missing.'

Another handshake. The Los Angeles sun is already hot. It had been a good forty minutes.

20 Things That Might Have Been

> 'Sinatra would have been so much better
> than the guy who played it, Omar Sharif,
> who's a wonderful actor, but no musical
> animal. You have to be a musical animal
> in a musical.'
>
> Jule Styne

Sinatra and Streisand, Sinatra and Julie Andrews – Sinatra even as *Dirty Harry*! It all sounded so promising, almost as if Sinatra was starting on screen career mark two. He was almost fifty years old. He had a lot of acting – and singing – left in him. The offers were enticing. The musicals it seemed were opening up again. Sadly it proved to be a false dawn. The offers were made in good faith, they just didn't materialize. Sinatra was left with the recurring thought, 'If only?'

The idea that he should team with Barbra Streisand came from Jule Styne. Along with lyricist Bob Merrill, Styne had written the score for the Broadway hit *Funny Girl* which dealt with the life and career of Fanny Brice. Streisand had become a star with her portrait of Brice. There was no question that she would repeat her role on screen. The part that was up for grabs was that of her gambler husband Nicky Arnstein. Styne wanted Sinatra. It was a dream he had long treasured. He said:

I kept saying to myself, what a combination! I mentioned it to Sinatra. He liked the idea, wanted to talk some more. Then I talked with the film's producer Ray Stark. He wasn't so sure. He said that Nicky Arnstein should be like a character out of a fairy tale and that Sinatra looked like the boy next door. Well, Sinatra hardly looks like the boy next door. When he walks on stage in his tuxedo millions of people aren't thinking he's the boy next door. Everyone is saying, this guy's *untouchable*!

Anyway, Sinatra was still interested. He had me go down to Vegas to discuss it some more. I sat with him for four hours. In the end he said, 'I'll do it. I know it's the girl's show. I'm resigned to that but I'll need a couple of new songs. We talked about some of the things that we might add to the score. He said, 'I don't know the girl. I've never met her. But she's tremendous.'

So, I had it all lined up and then it didn't happen. Stark wouldn't go for it. I pleaded with him but he didn't want to know. When he heard the news Sinatra thought *I* didn't want him, that *I'd* changed my mind. He wouldn't believe that it was Ray Stark who didn't want him. It cost me two years of Sinatra's friendship that damned thing.

Sinatra would have been so much better than the guy who played it, Omar Sharif, who's a wonderful actor but no musical animal. You have to be a musical animal in a musical. I still can't believe it didn't happen. Can you imagine Sinatra and Streisand together on one album. It would have been the collector's item of all time!

So too, for that matter, would any album featuring Sinatra and Julie Andrews and in 1964 that seemed a distinct possibility as producer Arthur Freed set about making his last ever MGM musical, *Say It With Music*. Metro had all but given up on the *genre* but Freed was determined to go out on a high note with a tribute to the music of Irving Berlin, a cavalcade that would start in the present and then regress to his sophisticated songs of *The Music Box Revue* days and end with the ragtime period, when Berlin's career had first got under way.

Freed's enthusiasm got the better of him. The reason MGM had given up producing original musicals in the first place was the cost. They estimated that anything that cost upwards of $2.5 million to $3 million dollars would not make a profit. There was no way they could get their money back after that. *Say It With Music* was going to cost twice, three times that, maybe more. They considered pulling the plug.

As a sop, Freed brought in director Vincente Minnelli who had made the studio's two Academy Award-winning musicals of the fifties, *An American In Paris* and *Gigi*. The studio were pacified for a while but after six months again began to grumble about the spiralling finance. Freed, who once had more musical clout than any producer in Hollywood, named Sinatra and Julie Andrews as his leads. Once again the studio let things ramble on. All told, Freed and Minnelli worked on the script for a year and a half. The film, like their enthusiasm, continued to grow in size and splendour. In the end, they had the piece climaxed by a ragtime ballet that incorporated symbols of the period – Frankie and Johnny's revolver, player pianos, card-playing, Derby hats and sleeve garters, soubrettes and honky-tonks.

Sinatra would occasionally call to ask how things were going to which Freed and Minnelli, with fingers crossed, would say enthusiastically, 'fine!'. Sinatra, who was beginning to wonder if the film would ever get off the ground, asked if they were sure everything was fine. They'd been working on the script for months and Metro hadn't even approached him to sign a contract for the picture. Julie Andrews too was waiting. She hadn't signed anything either.

Freed and Minnelli felt the storm clouds gathering. In the end, the studio took one look at the budget and decided enough was enough. They pulled the plug once again, this time for good. Freed and Minnelli had no more aces up their sleeves. The front office explained that the budget was out of control. Even with Sinatra and Andrews they couldn't be sure they'd make a profit. Freed retired from movies a disappointed man and Minnelli left MGM for good.

Sinatra was left high and dry with what can best be called the dregs – a hammy western called *Four For Texas*, a puerile comedy with Deborah Kerr, *Marriage On The Rocks*, an adventure yarn, *Assault On A Queen* and a spy thriller, *The Naked Runner*. He did star in and direct a cheap-budgeted anti-war movie called *None But The Brave* but that didn't really work out. Just about the only one that did was a POW escape thriller, *Von Ryan's Express*, which at least proved that he still had commercial clout.

It was a very different scene from the fifties when, at Oscar time, Sinatra's name was frequently being bandied about, either as an actor or as a singer of nominated songs. In the sixties, only 'My Kind Of Town' earned a best song nomination. There were

141

no acting honours. Of the roles that won Academy Awards for actors, only the bigoted small-town Southern sheriff played by Rod Steiger in *In The Heat Of The Night* might conceivably have been played by Sinatra.

The best offers, when they did come, arrived late in the decade from the Fox studio. Sinatra signed a three-picture deal to make a couple of private-eye movies, *Tony Rome* and *Lady In Cement*, and a version of Roderick Thorp's best-selling novel *The Detective*. On the face of it, it seemed just like any other deal. A couple of potboilers and a crime movie, the kind of thing many actors took on when the going got tough. It turned out to be more rewarding than that. For the first time in five years Sinatra actually looked as though he was enjoying himself on screen. As one critic noted, 'Sinatra has been a talent searching for a role since *The Manchurian Candidate* and at last he has found one, a type moulded by Bogart, a man with lines about the eyes, a way of walking and a used, hardened persona suggestive of integrity worn paper thin.'

He wasn't the first singer to have undergone such a transformation. In 1944 the guys down Raymond Chandler's mean streets had knocked the hell out of Dick Powell in *Farewell My Lovely*. Sinatra got the same treatment. It scarcely mattered whether he was investigating the disappearance of an heiress or trying to discover why a naked girl was found floating off the Florida coast with her feet encased in cement. The end result was invariably the same – a seduction by a *femme fatale* or a beating by the heavies. In one scene in *Lady In Cement* he is so amusingly inept at the rough stuff that the giant Dan Blocker picks him up as if he is a doll and places him in a sitting position on a bar. When he constantly asks himself why he is doing all this the answer is always the same. He has an impatient bookmaker.

The films were advertised with the tag line: HE'S A RELUCTANT PRIVATE EYE. HIS SCENE IS MIAMI BEACH WHERE SOME PEOPLE GET UP WHEN THE SUN SETS AND SOME NEVER GET UP AT ALL. It was the setting as much as the convoluted plots that made the Tony Rome films attractive. Miami, at that time, had not been used extensively as a locale for movies. With his Panavision cameras and some stunning colourwork, director Gordon Douglas made the most of what he had, tracking across the beaches and through the flop houses, luxury hotels and palatial mansions of the Florida resort.

Sinatra, for his part, enlivened every scene in which he appeared, working his way through all the dope addicts, crooked night-club owners, lesbian strippers and good-hearted lushes that crossed his path. Audiences didn't really care about what was going on. The complex plots would unravel in their own good time. They simply enjoyed watching a laconic Sinatra following in the footsteps of Bogart and Powell, lacing everything with a well-timed wisecrack and bringing to life an ordinary guy who may have looked as though he had it made aboard a cabin cruiser but who, at the end of the day, was just glad to come out a few bucks ahead.

The Detective was a much more serious affair and here Sinatra was even more impressive as a homicide detective who is one of life's sufferers – a man who has been used by life, thoroughly disenchanted by it and yet still manages to retain some ideals in a world gone rotten.

The film hinges on two apparently unrelated crimes – the murder of a homosexual (graphically described in a brutally realistic opening scene) and an apparent suicide. Gradually the strands of both crimes are woven together to reveal a corruption that is rife in the New York police force, a corruption that for many is best ignored. Sinatra's Joe Leland refuses to turn a blind eye to the dishonesty around him. A detective isolated by his principles, his idealism brings him in constant conflict with his superiors and with the repressive role of the police in urban society. In the end, having uncovered a conspiracy in the city government, he also finds a fatal flaw in himself. By revealing both, his police career is ended.

The film was a forerunner of many seventies cop movies that exposed corruption among the police, the most notable being Sidney Lumet's *Serpico*. As such it deserves a higher place in movie history than it usually receives.

Abby Mann's brilliantly economical screenplay and Gordon Douglas's craftsmanlike direction allowed Sinatra more chances than he'd been offered all decade. He seized them with both hands. A London critic enthused:

Mr Sinatra is the embodiment of the cop Joe Leland. This is the

role he has been waiting for for several years. He has been
sleep-walking through parts for too long. There aren't many
actors around these days who can take over the mantle of Bogart.
Sinatra isn't Bogart but he's the best thing we have. Let's hope
the film and the performance are the forerunners of many more
good things to come.

The Detective and *The Manchurian Candidate* emerged as the
best celluloid offerings of an otherwise disappointing decade for
Sinatra. Disappointing not only in what he failed to achieve on
the movie screen but in his personal life as well. On 19 July 1966
he surprised friends, and shocked many, by marrying the young
elfin-like actress Mia Farrow, the daughter of Maureen
O'Sullivan and director John Farrow. He was 50 and she was
21. 'It won't last' came the familiar cry. Those who uttered it
were correct. Sixteen months all told. He got tired of her, she
got bored with him. It ended in acrimony. The grounds for
divorce were inevitable – incompatibility.

Many said that Sinatra would have done better to have
married her widowed mother, the still beautiful Maureen.
Closer friends felt that he still hadn't got over Ava even though
there had been romances with such well-known actresses as
Lauren Bacall, Dorothy Provine and the young Juliet Prowse
whom he met on the set of *Can-Can*. In the end he did marry
again, in 1976 when he wed Barbara Marx, the former wife of
Zeppo Marx. They married in Palm Springs and have remained
together ever since.

By then Sinatra had announced his retirement from both the
screen and his music and had already made a comeback. Two
years was the most he could stay away. He has never been away
since – at least not from his recordings and concerts and tours.
With his movies it was a different story. In 1970 he made a
burlesque western called *Dirty Dingus Magee*. It flopped. 'All the
good roles seem to have been used up,' he lamented shortly
afterwards. 'There's nothing that's very challenging anymore.'
Don Siegel offered him another cop in his detective thriller
Dirty Harry. Sinatra was interested. Siegel was an accomplished
director. They got together. Four scripts were written. The film
was set in New York. In the end Sinatra backed off. Siegel said
he had cut his hand badly and couldn't make the starting date.
On the other hand Sinatra might just have been bored with

144

cops. A younger man was brought in. Clint Eastwood was in his early forties compared with Sinatra who was fifty-five. The locale was changed to San Francisco and Sinatra missed saying 'Go ahead punk, make my day!' It would have been interesting to see how he would have handled the line although it's quite possible it might not have been in the film's original scripts.

Other than a couple of other cop movies, one for TV (*Contract on Cherry Street*), the other for the cinema (*The First Deadly Sin*) that was about it. There were the occasional guest appearances and also a return to MGM as one of the presenters of the musical compilation *That's Entertainment*. But from 1973 onwards it was basically music, music, music.

Luckily, the advent of video in the last twenty years has meant that many of Sinatra's concerts and TV appearances have been recorded on cassette to be enjoyed at leisure, time and time again, in the home. They have been complemented by a four-hour TV film of his life, produced by his daughter Tina which rattled through the key events of his career without adding much to what was already known. As far as his movie career was concerned, the coverage of Sinatra's films was lamentable. The one saving grace was the performance of Philip Casnoff who caught to perfection Sinatra's gestures and mannerisms in a cleverly shaded portrayal.

At fifty-five years old, Sinatra was really much too young to retire from movies. It was a pity that, when he announced his retirement in 1971 and just two years later bounced back with the album *Ol' Blue Eyes Is Back*, he didn't bounce back with equal vigour into the movie world. But then one can't have everything. There had, after all, been nearly sixty films. It was enough to be going on with.

21   The Natural

'Frank is a super superstar. He has it. He
has the magic. He was at his peak in an
age of heavyweights.'

George Sidney

So, just how good an actor was he? Solid, dependable,
aggressive with occasional moments of brilliance or something
more? Fifty-nine movies should have provided some sort of an
answer but, as with all natural actors, the answer is not always
clear cut or easy to define. It's the word 'natural' that is the key.
Like others adorned with the description, Sinatra knew how to
play to the cameras. He knew exactly what was needed without
having to be told. He played himself, working his way through
his roles by using his own personality and relying as much on
instinct and intuition as any method of study. He had it, he
flaunted it and it worked!

When he was in the mood he could show a clean pair of heels
to anyone who dared to share a scene with him. On occasion he
traded blow for blow and scene for scene with the likes of Tracy
and Clift and Brando. Never once did he come out a loser. At
other times he would breeze through a role as if he didn't give a
cuss about what he was doing. Most of the time he got away with
it. Sometimes, though, it showed and it was then that he
infuriated his fans. A Sinatra film never seemed to reach down
into the darkness the way the songs did. Sinatra never cheated
on songs as he so often appeared to do with his films.

Critic Pauline Kael was one who was often incensed by his
lack of application. 'Why,' she asked, 'has Sinatra not developed

the professional pride in his movies that he takes in his recordings?' *New York Times* critic Bosley Crowther felt the same way, 'Sinatra's range and vitality as an entertainer are a phenomenon. That's why it's so provoking, nay disturbing and depressing beyond belief, to see this acute and awesome figure turning up time and time again in strangely trashy motion pictures.'

In the end, when assessing Sinatra's film career, one is left not so much with a collection of fine movies – although there are several that rank with Hollywood's best – more a series of moments that reflect the Sinatra charisma on screen. The moments are usually brief, almost elusive, but they are always spellbinding.

The scene in *The Joker Is Wild* for instance, as he stops momentarily behind a screen and listens wistfully to Crosby crooning 'June in January'; the self-pity poured into the piano ballads in *Young At Heart*; the seduction of Grace Kelly with 'You're Sensational' in *High Society*; the bounce and verve and sheer versatility as he goes *On The Town* with Kelly and company.

Then the exhilarating moments in *Pal Joey* as he delivers Rodgers and Hart as if he were at Las Vegas and the movie audience was at a ringside table: 'I Didn't Know What Time It Was'; 'There's a Small Hotel'; 'The Lady is a Tramp' – *pow, pow, pow*! One is left reeling.

And the more dramatic scenes; desperate for a fix in *The Man With The Golden Arm*; suffering traumatic nightmares in *The Manchurian Candidate*; clashing with stockade sergeant Ernest Borgnine in *From Here To Eternity*; troubled beyond belief as he realizes to his horror that he has sent an innocent man to the electric chair in *The Detective*.

These are but a few of the Sinatra moments that have graced the screens over the years.

Those who have worked with him, behind the cameras, to help create those scenes have mostly had a love-hate relationship with the actor. They have found him to be a Jekyll and Hyde character, sometimes up, frequently down, liable to explode without warning.

Lewis Milestone who directed him in the Rat Pack caper *Ocean's Eleven* found him easy going but moody. He quickly discovered that if you worked with Sinatra it was up to the director to understand his star. Sinatra was not going to put himself out to understand his director. 'I like a lot of things about the man,' said Milestone. 'He's temperamental, however, and if you line up twelve people who know him, you'll get twelve different versions of his character and behaviour.'

Screenwriter and novelist W.R. Burnett, a veteran of the great Warner days of the thirties and forties, was one who held very definite views on Sinatra. He couldn't believe anyone could be so careless and haphazard when making a movie. Sinatra had taken him to lunch and told him that he wanted to take the *Gunga Din* story and kid it. Would Burnett be interested in writing the screenplay? Burnett thought it was a good idea and proposed that the story might make a good spoof western. Sinatra agreed and Burnett went away to write the first draft. The producer, Howard Koch, took the draft to Vegas for Sinatra to check it through. He never got to see him. He spoke to him only on the telephone. 'Frank, what do you want us to do?'

'Write the script,' said Sinatra.

'But Burney's written it. I've got it here.'

'Yeah! Yeah! What to do you think Howard?'

'I think it's swell.'

'Fine, let's go.'

Burnett was flabbergasted. He'd written just one draft and that was the one they were going to use. 'It scared the hell out of me,' he said later.

Directors Frank Capra and George Sidney both had views on Sinatra as a star and as an entertainer. Capra worked with him just the once, Sidney on several occasions. Said Capra, 'He's a once in a lifetime star. That's exactly what he is – a superstar. Brighter than anyone. Bigger than he thinks he is – and it scares him; makes him mean at times. Champagne explodes when you bottle it in beer bottles!'

George Sidney who has known him for almost fifty years, sums him up thus:

Frank is one of those persons who, when the money's down and the race goes he comes out the winner ... I always liken him to a rubber ball, the lowest point you throw it at a wall it will come

148

back to you at a higher trajectory than before. It happened in his career. He's had more ups and downs than the British film industry and its amazing how he always manages to rise. We use the word superstar nowadays. Frank is a super superstar. He has it. He has the magic. He was at his peak in an age of heavyweights.

Director Vincente Minnelli claimed that Sinatra could be as feisty as a rooster and capable of towering rages and also the greatest of all foul-weather friends in the up and down business of movie making.

His most abiding memory of the actor was when he was making a film at Metro and needed to use a certain song on the soundtrack. Sinatra was not in the picture but Minnelli knew he could help in clearing the rights to the song. Minnelli himself was having some difficulty so he called Sinatra who was in the Orient. Minnelli explained the position. Sinatra cut him off halfway through. 'Don't worry,' he said. 'It is yours.' Minnelli, grateful that he had cut through so much red tape, began to thank him. Sinatra again interrupted, stressing each of the three words: '*It is yours*' Minnelli said: 'I wasn't on the phone with him for more than three minutes but before I'd hung up, the cogs had already started moving to get permission to use that song.'

Sinatra's longtime friend and colleague, director Gordon Douglas who worked with him more than any other film-maker, summed him up simply, 'To me, he's the king. I'm a sucker for Sinatra. He's exciting to be around. He's electricity. He sparks. He knows his dialogue and just what a scene's about. For me, he's one helluva guy.'

Gordon Douglas, who died in 1993, was one of those film-makers who never came close to winning an Academy Award for his work on feature films but he knew just how to get the best out of Sinatra and that was worth an award in itself, especially as he managed it not once but five times. And as awards have figured frequently in the pages of this book it might be appropriate to close its pages with three personal Oscars for Sinatra, all of them awarded for categories in which Sinatra excelled and all of them announced by strict Academy rules.

The best song? The five nominees: 'The Tender Trap', 'My Kind Of Town'; 'All The Way'; 'I Fall In Love Too Easily' and

Iアイ

'Time After Time'.

And the winner: 'The Tender Trap', music by James Van Heusen, lyrics by Sammy Cahn. Vintage, 1955.

The best performance? The five nominees: Maggio in *From Here to Eternity*; Joe Leland in *The Detective*; Bennett Marco in *The Manchurian Candidate*; Frankie Machine in *The Man With The Golden Arm*; Joe E. Lewis in *The Joker Is Wild*.

And the winner: Sinatra as Frankie Machine in *The Man With The Golden Arm*.

And finally, the best film. The nominees: *The Detective; From Here to Eternity; On The Town; The Man With The Golden Arm; The Manchurian Candidate*.

The winner? By a nose from *Eternity* and *On The Town*, *The Manchurian Candidate*.

Only a game of course, but one that you may care to play as you browse through the pages of Sinatra credits that follow this chapter. It's almost certain that you will arrive at different songs, different performances and different winners but the game, if nothing else, serves a purpose for it illustrates all that's best about Sinatra on screen during the last fifty years. In my introduction I mentioned that Sinatra's career had been something of a roller-coaster ride. The last 150 pages have, I hope, allowed you to relive the peaks and troughs and excitements of that ride and also allowed some insights into a world when movies used to be fun and the only four-letter words in a Sinatra film used to be three-letter ones called 'bum'. Things have changed but luckily, the movies remain.

Filmography

LAS VEGAS NIGHTS (1941)
Paramount: 89 minutes
Producer: William LeBaron. *Director*: Ralph Murphy. *Original screenplay*: Ernest Pagano and Harry Clark. *Photography*: William C. Mellor. *Musical Director*: Victor Young. Musical numbers staged by LeRoy Prinz. *Leading Players*: Constance Moore, Bert Wheeler, Phil Regan, Lillian Cornell, Virginia Dale, Hank Ladd, Tommy Dorsey and his Orchestra with male soloist Frank Sinatra
Sinatra's song: 'I'll Never Smile Again' by Ruth Lowe

SHIP AHOY (1942)
MGM: 95 minutes
Producer: Jack Cummings. *Director*: Edward Buzzell. *Screenplay*: Harry Clork. Additional material by Harry Kurnitz and Irving Brecher, based on a story by Matt Brooks, Bradford Ropes and Bert Kalmar. *Photography*: Leonard Smith and Robert Planck. Music supervised and conducted by George Stoll. Musical arrangements by Axel Stordahl, Sy Oliver, Leo Arnaud, George Bassman, Basil Adlam. *Leading Players*: Eleanor Powell, Red Skelton, Bert Lahr, Virginia O'Brien, William Post, jun., James Cross, Tommy Dorsey and his Orchestra with male vocalist Frank Sinatra
Sinatra's songs: 'The Last Call For Love' by Burton Lane, E.Y. Harburg and Margery Cummings, and 'Poor You' by Burton Lane and E.Y. Harburg

REVEILLE WITH BEVERLY (1943)
Columbia: 78 minutes
Producer: Sam White. *Director*: Charles Barton. *Original screenplay*: Howard J. Green, Jack Henley and Albert Duffy. *Photography*: Philip Tannura. *Musical Director*: Morris Stoloff. *Leading Players*: Ann Miller,

William Wright, Dick Purcell, Franklin Pangborn, Tim Ryan, Larry Parks; Bob Crosby and his Orchestra, Freddie Slack and his Orchestra, with Ella Mae Morse, Duke Ellington and his Orchestra, Count Basie and his Orchestra, Frank Sinatra, The Mills Brothers, The Radio Rogues
Sinatra's song: 'Night And Day' by Cole Porter

HIGHER AND HIGHER (1943)
RKO Radio: 90 minutes
Producer and Director: Tim Whelan. *Screenplay*: Jay Dratler and Ralph Spence. *Additional dialogue*: William Bowers and Howard Harris. Based on the play by Gladys Hurlbut and Joshua Logan. *Photography*: Robert DeGrasse *Musical Director*: Constantin Bakaleinikoff. *Orchestral arrangements*: Gene Rose. *Musical arrangements for Frank Sinatra*: Alex Stordahl. *Leading Players*: Michele Morgan, Jack Haley, Frank Sinatra, Leon Errol, Marcy McGuire, Victor Borge, Mary Wickes, Elisabeth Risdon, Barbara Hale. *Sinatra's songs*: 'You Belong In A Love Song'; 'I Couldn't Sleep A Wink Last Night' (Oscar nominated); 'A Lovely Way To Spend An Evening'; 'The Music Stopped' and 'I Saw You First' (all by Jimmy McHugh and Harold Adamson)

STEP LIVELY (1944)
RKO: 88 minutes
Producer: Robert Fellows. *Director*: Tim Whelan. *Screenplay*: Warren Duff and Peter Milne. Based on the play 'Room Service' by John Murray and Allen Boretz. *Photography*: Robert DeGrasse. *Musical Director*: Constantin Bakaleinikoff. *Orchestral arrangements*: Gene Rose. *Musical arrangements for Frank Sinatra:* Alex Stordahl. *Vocal arrangements*: Ken Darby. *Leading Players*: Frank Sinatra, George Murphy, Adolphe Menjou, Gloria De Haven, Walter Slezak, Eugene Pallette
Sinatra's songs: 'Come Out, Come Out, Wherever You Are'; 'Where Does Love Begin?'; 'As Long as There's Music' and 'Some Other Time' (all by Jule Styne and Sammy Cahn)

ANCHORS AWEIGH (1945)
MGM: 143 minutes
Producer: Joe Pasternak. *Director*: George Sidney. *Screenplay*: Isobel Lennart. Based on a story by Natalie Marcin. *Photography*: Robert Planck and Charles Boyle (*Technicolor*). Music supervised and conducted by George Stoll. Frank Sinatra's vocal arrangements by Alex Stordahl. Dance sequences created by Gene Kelly. *Leading*

Players: Frank Sinatra, Kathryn Grayson, Gene Kelly, Jose Iturbi, Dean Stockwell, Pamela Britton, Rags Ragland, Billy Gilbert, Henry O'Neill
Sinatra's songs: 'We Hate To Leave'; 'What Makes The Sunset?'; 'The Charm Of You'; 'I Begged Her'; 'I Fall in Love Too Easily' (Oscar nominated) – all by Jule Styne and Sammy Cahn; 'Lullaby' by Johannes Brahms

THE HOUSE I LIVE IN (1945)
RKO Radio: 10 minutes
Producer: Frank Ross. *Director*: Mervyn LeRoy. *Original screenplay*: Albert Maltz. *Editor*: Philip Martin, Jr. *Musical Director*: Alex Stordahl.
Leading Player: Frank Sinatra
Sinatra's songs: 'If You Are But A Dream' by Nathan J. Bonx, Jack Fulton and Moe Jaffe' (adapted from Anton Rubinstein's 'Romance') and 'The House I Live In' by Earl Robinson and Lewis Allan

TILL THE CLOUDS ROLL BY (1946)
MGM: 137 minutes
Producer: Arthur Freed. *Director*: Richard Whorf. *Screenplay*: Myles Connolly and Jean Holloway. Adapted by George Wells from an original story by Guy Bolton. Based on the life and music of Jerome Kern. *Photography (Technicolor)*: Harry Stradling and George Folsey. Music supervised and conducted by Lennie Hayton. Orchestrations by Conrad Salinger. Musical numbers staged and directed by Robert Alton. *Leading Players*: June Allyson, Lucille Bremer, Judy Garland, Kathryn Grayson, Van Heflin, Lena Horne, Van Johnson, Angela Lansbury, Tony Martin, Virginia O'Brien, Dinah Shore, Frank Sinatra, Robert Walker
Sinatra's song: 'Ol' Man River' by Jerome Kern and Oscar Hammerstein II

IT HAPPENED IN BROOKLYN (1947)
MGM: 104 minutes
Producer: Jack Cummings. *Director*: Richard Whorf. *Screenplay*: Isobel Lennart. Based on an original story by John McGowan. *Photography*: Robert Planck. Musical supervision, direction and incidental score by Johnny Green. Frank Sinatra's vocal orchestrations by Axel Stordahl.
Leading Players: Frank Sinatra, Kathryn Grayson, Peter Lawford, Jimmy Durante, Gloria Grahame, Marcy McGuire, Aubrey Mather
Sinatra's songs: 'Brooklyn Bridge'; 'I Believe'; 'Time After Time'; 'The Song's Gotta Come from the Heart' and 'It's The Same Old Dream' (all by Jule Styne and Sammy Cahn); 'La Ci Darem la Mano' by

Mozart; 'Black Eyes' (Russian)

THE MIRACLE OF THE BELLS (1948)
RKO Radio: 120 minutes
Producers: Jesse L. Lasky and Walter MacEwen. *Director*: Irving Pichel. *Screenplay*: Ben Hecht and Quentin Reynolds. Additional material for Frank Sinatra's sequences by DeWitt Bodeen. Based on the novel by Russell Janney. *Photography*: Robert De Grasse. *Musical Director*: C. Bakaleinikoff. *Leading Players*: Fred MacMurray, Alida Valli, Frank Sinatra, Lee J. Cobb, Harold Vermilye, Charles Meredith, Jim Nolan
Sinatra's song: 'Ever Homeward' by Kasimierz Lubomirski, Jule Styne and Sammy Cahn.

THE KISSING BANDIT (1948)
MGM: 102 minutes
Producer: Joe Pasternak. *Director*: Laslo Benedek. *Original screenplay*: Isobel Lennart and John Briard Harding. *Photography (Technicolor)*: Robert Surtees. Music supervised and conducted by George Stoll. Incidental score by George Stoll, Albert Sendrey, Scott Bradley and Andre Previn. *Dance direction*: Stanley Donen. *Leading players*: Frank Sinatra, Kathryn Grayson. J. Carrol Naish, Mildred Natwick, Mikhail Rasumny, Billy Gilbert, Sono Osato, Clinton Sundberg – and Ricardo Montalban, Ann Miller and Cyd Charisse
Sinatra's songs: 'What's Wrong with Me?' 'If I Steal a Kiss' and 'Senorita' (all by Nacio Herb Brown and Edward Heyman); 'Siesta' by Nacio Herb Brown and Earl Brent

TAKE ME OUT TO THE BALL GAME (1949)
(EVERYBODY'S CHEERING: UK)
MGM: 93 minutes
Producer: Arthur Freed. *Director*: Busby Berkeley. *Screenplay*: Harry Tugend and George Wells based on a story by Gene Kelly and Stanley Donen. *Photography (Technicolor)*: George Folsey. Music supervised and conducted by Adolph Deutsch. *Incidental score*: Roger Edens. *Vocal arrangements*: Robert Tucker. *Dance direction*: Gene Kelly and Stanley Donen. *Leading players*: Frank Sinatra, Esther Williams, Gene Kelly, Betty Garrett, Edward Arnold, Jules Munshin, Richard Lane, Tom Dugan
Sinatra's songs: 'Take Me Out To The Ball Game' by Albert von Tilzer and Jack Norworth; 'Yes, Indeedy', 'O'Brien to Ryan to Goldberg', 'The Right Girl For Me' and 'It's Fate, Baby, It's Fate' – all by Roger Edens, Betty Comden and Adolph Green: 'Strictly USA' by Roger Edens

ON THE TOWN (1949)
MGM: 98 minutes
Producer: Arthur Freed. *Directors*: Gene Kelly and Stanley Donen. *Screenplay*: Adolph Green and Betty Comden, from their musical play based on an idea by Jerome Robbins. *Photography (Technicolor)*: Harold Rosson. Music supervised and conducted by Lennie Hayton. *Incidental score*: Roger Edens, Saul Chaplin, Conrad Salinger. Music for 'Miss Turnstiles' and 'A Day In New York' by Leonard Bernstein. *Leading players*: Gene Kelly, Frank Sinatra, Betty Garrett, Ann Miller, Jules Munshin, Vera-Ellen, Florence Bates, Alice Pearce, George Meader
Sinatra's songs: 'New York, New York' and 'Come Up To My Place' by Leonard Bernstein, Adolph Green and Betty Comden: 'You're Awful', 'On The Town', and 'Count on Me' by Roger Edens, Adolph Green and Betty Comden

DOUBLE DYNAMITE (1951)
RKO Radio: 80 minutes
Producer: Irving Cummings Jun. *Director*: Irving Cummings. *Screenplay* by Melville Shavelson. Additional dialogue by Harry Crane. From an original story by Leo Rosten, based on a character created by Mannie Manheim. *Photography*: Robert DeGrasse. *Music*: Leigh Harline. *Leading players*: Jane Russell, Groucho Marx, Frank Sinatra, Don McGuire, Howard Freeman, Nestor Paiva, Frank Orth, Harry Hayden, William Edmunds, Russell Thorson
Sinatra's songs: 'Kisses and Tears' and 'It's Only Money' – both by Jule Styne and Sammy Cahn

MEET DANNY WILSON (1951)
Universal International: 88 minutes
Producer: Leonard Goldstein. *Director*: Joseph Pevney. *Original screenplay*: Don McGuire. *Photography*: Maury Gertsman. *Musical director*: Joseph Gershenson. Musical numbers staged by Hal Belfer. *Leading players*: Frank Sinatra, Shelley Winters, Alex Nicol, Raymond Burr, Tommy Farrell, Vaughn Taylor, Donald McBride, Barbara Knudson
Sinatra's songs: 'You're a Sweetheart' by Jimmy McHugh and Harold Adamson; 'Lonesome Man Blues' by Sy Oliver; 'She's Funny that Way' by Richard Whiting and Neil Moret; 'A Good Man Is Hard To Find' by Eddie Green; 'That Old Black Magic' by Harold Arlen and Johnny Mercer; 'When You're Smiling' by Mark Fisher, Joe Goodwin and Larry Shay; 'All Of Me' by Seymour Simons and Gerald Marks; 'I've Got A Crush On You' by George and Ira Gershwin; 'How Deep Is The Ocean?' by Irving Berlin

FROM HERE TO ETERNITY (1953)
Columbia: 118 minutes
Producer: Buddy Adler. *Director*: Fred Zinnemann. *Screenplay*: Daniel Taradash, based on the novel by James Jones. *Photography*: Burnett Guffey. Music supervised and conducted by Morris Stoloff. *Background music*: George Duning. *Leading players*: Burt Lancaster, Montgomery Clift, Deborah Kerr, Donna Reed, Frank Sinatra, Philip Ober, Mickey Shaughnessy, Harry Bellaver, Ernest Borgnine, Jack Warden, John Dennis, Merle Travis, Tim Ryan

SUDDENLY (1954)
United Artists: 77 minutes
Producer: Robert Bassler. *Director*: Lewis Allen. Original screenplay by Richard Sale. *Photography*: Charles G. Clarke. Music by David Raksin. *Leading players*: Frank Sinatra, Sterling Hayden, James Gleason, Nancy Gates, Willis Bouchey, Kim Charney, James Lilburn, Paul Frees, Christopher Dark

YOUNG AT HEART (1954)
Warner Brothers: 117 minutes
Producer: Henry Blanke. *Director*: Gordon Douglas. Adaptation by Liam O'Brien from the screenplay 'Four Daughters' by Julius J. Epstein and Lenore Coffee. Based on the 'Cosmopolitan' magazine story 'Sister Act' by Fannie Hurst. *Photography (Warnercolor)*: Ted McCord. Music supervised, arranged and conducted by Ray Heindorf. Piano solos by Andre Previn. *Leading players*: Doris Day, Frank Sinatra, Gig Young, Ethel Barrymore, Dorothy Malone, Robert Keith, Elisabeth Fraser, Alan Hale, Jun., Lonny Chapman
Sinatra's songs: 'Young At Heart' by Johnny Richards and Carolyn Leigh; 'Someone to Watch Over Me' by George and Ira Gershwin; 'Just One Of Those Things' by Cole Porter; 'One for My Baby' by Harold Arlen and Johnny Mercer; 'You, My Love' by Mack Gordon and James Van Heusen.

NOT AS A STRANGER (1955)
United Artists: 135 minutes
Producer and Director: Stanley Kramer. *Screenplay*: Edna and Edward Anhalt. Based on the novel by Morton Thompson. *Photography*: Franz Planer. *Music*: George Antheil. *Leading players*: Olivia de Havilland, Robert Mitchum, Frank Sinatra, Gloria Grahame, Broderick Crawford, Charles Bickford, Myron McCormick, Lon Chaney, Jesse White, Harry Morgan, Lee Marvin, Virginia Christine

THE TENDER TRAP (1955)
MGM: 111 minutes
Producer: Lawrence Weingarten. *Director*: Charles Walters. Screenplay by Julius J. Epstein. Based on the play by Max Shulman and Robert Paul Smith. *Photography (Eastman Color/CinemaScope)*: Paul C. Vogel. Music composed and conducted by Jeff Alexander. *Leading players*: Frank Sinatra, Debbie Reynolds, David Wayne, Celeste Holm, Jarma Lewis, Lola Albright, Carolyn Jones, Howard St. John
Sinatra's song: '(Love Is) The Tender Trap' (Oscar nominated) by James Van Heusen and Sammy Cahn

GUYS AND DOLLS (1955)
A Samuel Goldwyn Production, released by MGM: 150 minutes
Producer: Samuel Goldwyn. *Director*: Joseph L. Mankiewicz. *Screenplay*: Joseph L. Mankiewicz. From the musical play, book by Jo Swerling and Abe Burrows, music and lyrics by Frank Loesser. Based on the story 'The Idyll of Miss Sarah Brown' by Damon Runyon. *Photography (Eastman Color/CinemaScope)*: Harry Stradling. Music Supervised and conducted by Jay Blackton. Orchestral arrangements by Skip Martin, Nelson Riddle (for Sinatra), Alexander Courage and Albert Sendrey. *Leading players*: Marlon Brando, Jean Simmons, Frank Sinatra, Vivian Blaine, Robert Keith, Stubby Kaye, B.S. Pully, Johnny Silver, Sheldon Leonard, Dan Dayton, George E. Stone
Sinatra's songs: 'The Oldest Established (Permanent Floating Crap Game In New York): 'Guys and Dolls', 'Adelaide' and 'Sue Me' (all by Frank Loesser)

THE MAN WITH THE GOLDEN ARM (1955)
United Artists: 119 minutes
Producer and director: Otto Preminger. *Screenplay*: Walter Newman and Lewis Meltzer. Based on the novel by Nelson Algren. *Photography*: Sam Leavitt. *Music*: Elmer Bernstein. *Leading players*: Frank Sinatra, Eleanor Parker, Kim Novak, Arnold Stang, Darren McGavin, Robert Strauss, John Conte, Doro Merande, George E. Stone, George Mathews, Emile Meyer, Shelly Manne (as himself)

MEET ME IN LAS VEGAS (1956)
(VIVA LAS VEGAS! UK)
MGM: 112 minutes
Producer: Joe Pasternak. *Director*: Roy Rowland. Original screenplay by Isobel Lennart. *Photography (Eastman Color/CinemaScope)*: Robert

Bronner. Music supervised and conducted by George Stoll. *Leading players*: Dan Dailey, Cyd Charisse, Jerry Colonna, Paul Henreid, Lena Horne, Frankie Laine, Agnes Moorehead and unbilled guest stars Frank Sinatra, Debbie Reynolds, Tony Martin, Peter Lorre, Vic Damone, Elaine Stewart

JOHNNY CONCHO (1956)
United Artists: 84 minutes
Producer: Frank Sinatra. *Director*: Don McGuire. Screenplay by David P. Harmon and Don McGuire. Based on the story 'The Man Who Owned The Town' by David P. Harmon. *Photography*: William C. Mellor. Music composed and conducted by Nelson Riddle. *Leading players*: Frank Sinatra, Keenan Wynn, William Conrad, Phyllis Kirk, Wallace Ford, Christopher Dark, Howard Petrie, Harry Bartell

HIGH SOCIETY (1956)
MGM: 107 minutes
Producer: Sol C. Siegel. *Director*: Charles Walters Screenplay by John Patrick. Based on the play 'The Philadelphia Story' by Philip Barry. *Photography (Technicolor/VistaVision):* Paul C. Vogel. Music supervised and adapted by Johnny Green and Saul Chaplin. Orchestral arrangements by Conrad Salinger and Nelson Riddle. *Leading players*: Bing Crosby, Grace Kelly, Frank Sinatra, Celeste Holm, John Lund, Louis Calhern, Sidney Blackmer, Louis Armstrong, Margalo Gilmore, Lydia Reed
Sinatra's songs: 'Who Wants To Be A Millionaire?', 'You're Sensational', 'Well, Did You Evah?' and 'Mind If I Make Love to You?' – all by Cole Porter

AROUND THE WORLD IN EIGHTY DAYS (1956)
United Artists: 178 minutes
Producer: Michael Todd. *Director*: Michael Anderson. Screenplay by James Poe, John Farrow and S.J. Perelman. Based on the novel by Jules Verne. *Photography (Eastman Color/Todd-AO)*: Lionel Lindon. *Music*: Victor Young. *Leading players*: David Niven. Cantinflas, Shirley MacLaine, Robert Newton plus more than forty guest cameo performances among them Frank Sinatra

THE PRIDE AND THE PASSION (1957)
United Artists: 132 minutes
Producer and Director: Stanley Kramer. *Screenplay*: Edward and Edna Anhalt. Based on the novel 'The Gun' by C.S. Forester. *Photography (Technicolor/VistaVision)*: Franz Planer. *Music*: George Antheil;

orchestrated and conducted by Ernest Gold. *Leading players*: Cary Grant, Frank Sinatra, Sophia Loren, Theodore Bikel, John Wengraf, Jay Novello, Jose Nieto, Carlos Larranaga.

THE JOKER IS WILD (1957)
Paramount: 126 minutes
Producer: Samuel J. Briskin. *Director*: Charles Vidor. Screenplay by Oscar Saul. Based on the book by Art Cohn. *Photography (VistaVision)*: Daniel L. Fapp. Music composed and conducted by Walter Scharf. *Orchestrations*: Leo Shuken and Jack Hayes. *Orchestration of songs*: Nelson Riddle. *Leading players*: Frank Sinatra, Mitzi Gaynor, Jeanne Crain, Eddie Albert, Beverly Garland, Jackie Coogan, Barry Kelley, Ted De Corsia. Sophie Tucker (as herself)
Sinatra's songs: 'I Cried for You' by Arthur Freed, Gus Arnheim and Abe Lyman; 'If I Could Be with You' by Jimmy Johnson and Henry Creamer; 'Chicago' by Fred Fisher; 'All The Way' (Oscar winner) by James Van Heusen and Sammy Cahn

PAL JOEY (1957)
Columbia: 111 minutes
Producer: Fred Kohlmar. *Director*: George Sidney. *Screenplay*: Dorothy Kingsley. Based on the musical play by John O'Hara (book), Richard Rodgers (music) and Lorenz Hart (lyrics). *Photography (Technicolor)*: Harold Lipstein. Music supervised and conducted by Morris Stoloff. Musical arrangements by Nelson Riddle. *Leading players*: Rita Hayworth, Frank Sinatra, Kim Novak, Barbara Nichols, Bobby Sherwood, Hank Henry, Elizabeth Patterson, Robin Morse
Sinatra's songs: 'I Didn't Know What Time It Was'; 'There's a Small Hotel'; 'I Could Write A Book'; 'The Lady Is A Tramp'; 'Bewitched, Bothered and Bewildered' and 'What Do I Care for a Dame' – all by Richard Rodgers and Lorenz Hart

KINGS GO FORTH (1958)
United Artists: 109 minutes
Producer: Frank Ross. *Director*: Delmer Daves. Screenplay by Merle Miller. Based on the novel by Joe David Brown. *Photography*: Daniel L. Fapp. *Music*: Elmer Bernstein. *Leading players*: Frank Sinatra, Tony Curtis, Natalie Wood, Leora Dana, Karl Swenson, Anne Codee, Edward Ryder, Jackie Berthe

SOME CAME RUNNING (1958)
MGM: 127 minutes
Producer: Sol C. Siegel. *Director*: Vincente Minnelli. Screenplay by

John Patrick and Arthur Sheekman. Based on the novel by James Jones. *Photography (Metrocolor/CinemaScope)*: William H. Daniels. *Music*: Elmer Bernstein. *Leading players*: Frank Sinatra, Dean Martin, Shirley MacLaine, Martha Hyer, Arthur Kennedy, Nancy Gates, Leora Dana, Betty Lou Keim, Carmen Phillips, Steven Peck, Connie Gilchrist

A HOLE IN THE HEAD (1959)
United Artists: 120 minutes
Producer and Director: Frank Capra. Screenplay by Arnold Schulman, based on his play. *Photography (DeLuxe/CinemaScope)*: William H. Daniels. Music by Nelson Riddle. *Leading players*: Frank Sinatra, Edward G. Robinson, Eleanor Parker, Carolyn Jones, Thelma Ritter, Keenan Wynn, Eddie Hodges
Sinatra's songs: 'All My Tomorrows' and 'High Hopes' (Oscar winner)-both by James Van Heusen and Sammy Cahn

NEVER SO FEW (1959)
MGM: 124 minutes
Producer: Edmund Grainger. *Director*: John Sturges. Screenplay by Millard Kaufman. Based on the novel by Tom T. Chamales. *Photography (MetroColor/CinemaScope)*: William H. Daniels. *Music*: Hugo Friedhofer. *Leading players*: Frank Sinatra, Gina Lollobrigida, Peter Lawford, Steve McQueen, Richard Johnson, Paul Henreid, Brian Donlevy, Dean Jones, Charles Bronson

CAN-CAN (1960)
20th Century-Fox: 130 minutes
Producer: Jack Cummings. *Director*: Walter Lang. Screenplay by Dorothy Kingsley and Charles Lederer. Based on the musical play by Abe Burrows. Songs by Cole Porter. *Photography (Technicolor/Todd-AO)*: William H. Daniels. Music arranged and conducted by Nelson Riddle. Vocal supervision by Bobby Tucker. Dances staged by Hermes Pan. *Leading players*: Frank Sinatra, Shirley MacLaine, Maurice Chevalier, Louis Jourdan, Juliet Prowse, Marcel Dalio, Leon Belasco, Nestor Paiva
Sinatra's songs: 'I Love Paris', 'C'est Magnifique', 'Let's Do It' and 'It's All Right with Me' – all by Cole Porter

OCEAN'S ELEVEN (1960)
Warner Brothers: 127 minutes
Producer and Director: Lewis Milestone. Screenplay by Harry Brown and Charles Lederer. Based on an original story by George Clayton Johnson and Jack Golden Russell. *Photography (Technicolor/Panavision)*: William

H. Daniels. Music composed and conducted by Nelson Riddle. Leading players: Frank Sinatra, Dean Martin, Sammy Davis Jun., Peter Lawford, Angie Dickinson, Richard Conte, Cesar Romero, Patrice Wymore, Joey Bishop, Akim Tamiroff, Henry Silva, Ilka Chase

PEPE (1960)
Columbia: 195 minutes
Producer and Director: George Sidney. Screenplay by Dorothy Kingsley and Claude Binyon. From a story by Leonard Spigelgass and Sonya Levien. Based on the play *Broadway Magic* by Ladislas Bush-Fekete. *Photography (Technicolor/sequences in CinemaScope)*: Joe MacDonald. *Music supervision and background score*: Johnny Green. *Leading players*: Cantinflas, Dan Dailey, Shirley Jones, Carlos Montalban, Vickie Trickett, Matt Mattox and 27 guest stars as themselves including Frank Sinatra

THE DEVIL AT FOUR O'CLOCK (1961)
Columbia: 126 minutes
Producer: Fred Kohlmar. *Director*: Mervyn LeRoy. Screenplay by Liam O'Brien. Based on the novel by Max Catto. *Photography (Eastman Color)*: Joseph Biroc. Music by George Duning. *Leading Players*: Spencer Tracy, Frank Sinatra, Kerwin Mathews, Jean Pierre Aumont, Gregoire Aslan, Alexander Scourby, Barbara Luna, Cathy Lewis

SERGEANTS THREE (1962)
United Artists: 112 minutes
Producer: Frank Sinatra. *Director*: John Sturges. Original screenplay by W.R. Burnett. *Photography (Technicolor/Panavision)*: Winton C. Hoch. Music by Billy May. *Leading players*: Frank Sinatra, Dean Martin, Sammy Davis Jun., Peter Lawford, Joe Bishop, Henry Silva, Ruta Lee, Buddy Lester, Phillip Crosby, Dennis Crosby, Lindsay Crosby

THE ROAD TO HONG KONG (1962)
United Artists: 91 minutes
Producer: Melvin Frank. *Director*: Norman Panama. Original screenplay by Norman Panama and Melvin Frank. *Photography*: Jack Hildyard. Music composed and conducted by Robert Farnon. *Leading players*: Bing Crosby, Bob Hope, Joan Collins, Dorothy Lamour, Robert Morley, Walter Gotell, Roger Delgardo, Felix Aylmer, Peter Madden and unbilled guest stars: Jerry Colonna, Dean Martin, David Niven, Peter Sellers, Frank Sinatra

THE MANCHURIAN CANDIDATE (1962)
United Artists: 126 minutes
Producers: George Axelrod and John Frankenheimer. *Director*: John Frankenheimer. Screenplay by George Axelrod. Based on the novel by Richard Condon. *Photography*: Lionel Lindon. Music composed and conducted by David Amram. *Leading players*: Frank Sinatra, Laurence Harvey, Janet Leigh, Angela Lansbury, Henry Silva, James Gregory, Leslie Parrish, John McGiver, Khigh Dhiegh, James Edwards, Douglas Henderson

COME BLOW YOUR HORN (1963)
Paramount: 112 minutes
Producers: Norman Lear and Bud Yorkin. *Director*: Bud Yorkin. Screenplay by Norman Lear. Based on the play by Neil Simon. *Photography (Technicolor/Panavision)*: William H. Daniels. Music composed and conducted by Nelson Riddle. *Leading players*: Frank Sinatra, Lee J. Cobb, Molly Picon, Barbara Rush, Jill St. John, Tony Bill, Dan Blocker, Phyllis McGuire, Herbie Faye
Sinatra's song: 'Come Blow Your Horn' by James Van Heusen and Sammy Cahn

THE LIST OF ADRIAN MESSENGER (1963)
Universal: 98 minutes
Producer: Edward Lewis. *Director*: John Huston. Screenplay by Anthony Veiller. Based on the novel by Philip MacDonald. *Photography*: Joe MacDonald. Music by Jerry Goldsmith. *Leading players*: George C. Scott, Dana Wynter, Clive Brook, Gladys Cooper, Herbert Marshall and guest stars Tony Curtis, Kirk Douglas, Burt Lancaster, Robert Mitchum and Frank Sinatra

4 FOR TEXAS (1964)
Warner Brothers: 124 minutes
Producer and Director: Robert Aldrich. Original screenplay by Teddi Sherman and Robert Aldrich. *Photography (Technicolor)*: Ernest Laszlo. Music composed and conducted by Nelson Riddle. *Leading players*: Frank Sinatra, Dean Martin, Anita Ekberg, Ursula Andress, Charles Bronson, Victor Buono, Edric Connor, Nick Dennis, Richard Jaeckel, Mike Mazurki, Wesley Addy

ROBIN AND THE SEVEN HOODS (1964)
Warner Brothers: 123 minutes
Producer: Frank Sinatra. *Director*: Gordon Douglas. Original screenplay by David R. Schwartz. *Photography (Technicolor/Panavision)*:

William H. Daniels. Music composed and conducted by Nelson Riddle. *Leading players*: Frank Sinatra, Dean Martin, Sammy Davis Jun., Peter Falk, Barbara Rush, Victor Buono, Hank Henry, Allen Jenkins, Jack La Rue, Robert Foulk
Sinatra's songs: 'My Kind of Town' (Oscar nominated), 'Style', 'Mr. Booze' and 'Don't Be a Do-Badder' – all by James Van Heusen and Sammy Cahn

NONE BUT THE BRAVE (1965)
Warner Brothers: 105 minutes
Producer and Director: Frank Sinatra. Screenplay by John Twist and Katsuya Susaki. *Photography (Technicolor/Panavision)*: Harold Lipstein. *Music*: Johnny Williams. *Leading players*: Frank Sinatra, Clint Walker, Tommy Sands, Brad Dexter, Tony Bill

VON RYAN'S EXPRESS (1965)
20th Century-Fox: 117 minutes
Producer: Saul David. *Director*: Mark Robson. Screenplay by Wendell Mayes and Joseph Landon. Based on the novel by David Westheimer. *Photography (DeLuxe Color/CinemaScope)*: William H. Daniels. Music by Jerry Goldsmith. *Leading players*: Frank Sinatra, Trevor Howard, Raffaella Carra, Brad Dexter, Sergio Fantoni, John Leyton, Edward Mulhare, Wolfgang Preiss, James Brolin.

MARRIAGE ON THE ROCKS (1965)
Warner Brothers: 109 minutes
Producer and Director of Photography (Technicolor/Panavision): William H. Daniels. *Director*: Jack Donohue. Original screenplay by Cy Howard. Music composed and conducted by Nelson Riddle. *Leading players*: Frank Sinatra, Deborah Kerr, Dean Martin, Cesar Romero, Hermione Baddeley, Tony Bill, John McGiver, Nancy Sinatra

CAST A GIANT SHADOW (1966)
United Artists: 139 minutes
Producer and Director: Melville Shavelson. *Screenplay*: Melville Shavelson. Based on the book by Ted Berkman. *Photography (DeLuxe Color/Panavision)*: Aldo Tonti. Music by Elmer Bernstein. *Leading players*: Kirk Douglas, Senta Berger, Angie Dickinson, James Donald, Stathis Giallelis, Luther Adler, Gary Merrill, Haym Topol and in guest cameos, Frank Sinatra, Yul Brynner and John Wayne

163

THE OSCAR (1966)
Embassy: 119 minutes
Producer: Clarence Greene. *Director*: Russell Rouse. Screenplay by Harlan Ellison, Russell Rouse and Clarence Green. Based on the novel by Richard Sale. *Photography (Pathe Color)*: Joseph Ruttenberg. Music by Percy Faith. *Leading players*: Stephen Boyd, Elke Sommer, Milton Berle, Eleanor Parker, Joseph Cotten, Jill St. John, Tony Bennett, Edie Adams, Ernest Borgnine, Ed Begley, Walter Brennan, (as themselves) Bob Hope and Frank Sinatra

ASSAULT ON A QUEEN (1966)
Paramount: 106 minutes
Producer: William Goetz. *Director*: Jack Donohue. Screenplay by Rod Serling. Based on the novel by Jack Finney. *Photography (Technicolor/ Panavision)*: William H. Daniels. Music by Duke Ellington. *Leading players*: Frank Sinatra, Virna Lisi, Tony Franciosa, Richard Conte, Alf Kjellin, Errol John, Murray Matheson, Reginald Denny, John Warburton

THE NAKED RUNNER (1967)
Warner Brothers: 103 minutes
Producer: Brad Dexter. *Director*: Sidney J. Furie. Screenplay by Stanley Mann. Based on the novel by Francis Clifford. *Photography (Technicolor/Techniscope)*: Otto Heller. Music by Harry Sukman. *Leading players*: Frank Sinatra, Peter Vaughan, Derren Nesbitt, Nadia Gray, Toby Robbins, Inger Stratton, Cyril Luckham, Edward Fox

TONY ROME (1967)
20th Century-Fox: 110 minutes
Producer: Aaron Rosenberg. *Director*: Gordon Douglas. Screenplay by Richard L. Breen. Based on the novel *Miami Mayhem* by Marvin H. Albert. *Photography (DeLuxe Color/Panavision)*: Joseph Biroc. Music by Billy May. *Leading players*: Frank Sinatra, Jill St. John, Richard Conte, Gena Rowlands, Simon Oakland, Jeffrey Lynn, Lloyd Bochner, Robert J. Wilke, Virginia Vincent

THE DETECTIVE (1968)
20th Century-Fox: 114 minutes
Producer: Aaron Rosenberg. *Director*: Gordon Douglas. Screenplay by Abby Mann. Based on the novel by Roderick Thorp. *Photography (DeLuxe Color/Panavision)*: Joseph Biroc. Music by Jerry Goldsmith. *Leading players*: Frank Sinatra, Lee Remick, Ralph Meeker, Jack

Klugman, Horace McMahon, Lloyd Bochner, William Windom, Tony Musante, Al Freeman Jun, Robert Duvall, Pat Henry

LADY IN CEMENT (1968)
20th Century-Fox: 93 minutes
Producer: Aaron Rosenberg. *Director*: Gordon Douglas. Screenplay by Marvin H. Albert and Jack Guss. Based on the novel by Marvin H. Albert. *Photography*: *(DeLuxe Color/Panavision)*: Joseph Biroc. Music composed and conducted by Hugo Montenegro. Orchestration by Billy May. *Leading players*: Frank Sinatra, Raquel Welch, Dan Blocker, Richard Conte, Martin Gabel, Lainie Kazan, Pat Henry, Steve Peck

DIRTY DINGUS MAGEE (1970)
MGM: 91 minutes
Producer and Director: Burt Kennedy. Screenplay by Tom and Frank Waldman and Joseph Heller. Based on the novel *The Ballad of Dingus Magee* by David Markson. *Photography (Metrocolor/Panavision)*: Harry Stradling, Jun. Music by Jeff Alexander and Billy Strange. *Leading players*: Frank Sinatra, George Kennedy, Anne Jackson, Lois Nettleton, Jack Elam, Michele Carey, John Dehner, Henry Jones, Harry Carey Jun.

THAT'S ENTERTAINMENT (1974)
MGM: 137 minutes
Production, Direction & Screenplay: Jack Haley, Jun. *Additional Photography (Metrocolor/70 mm)*: Gene Polito, Ernest Laszlo, Russell Metty, Ennio Guarnieri, Allan Green. Additional music & adaptation: Henry Mancini. *Narrators*: Fred Astaire, Bing Crosby, Gene Kelly, Peter Lawford, Liza Minnelli, Donald O'Connor, Debbie Reynolds, Mickey Rooney, Frank Sinatra, James Stewart, Elizabeth Taylor
In this montage film Sinatra is represented by extracts from five of his Metro films: *Take Me Out To The Ball Game, On The Town, Anchors Aweigh, High Society* and *It Happened in Brooklyn*. In the last sequence he appears singing a duet with Jimmy Durante, 'The Song's Gotta Come From The Heart'

CONTRACT ON CHERRY STREET (1977)
Columbia: 180 minutes
Television Movie
Producer: Hugh Benson. *Director*: William A. Graham. Teleplay by Edward Anhalt. Based on the book by Philip Rosenberg. *Photography (Color)*: *Jack Priestley*. *Music*: *Jerry Goldsmith*. *Leading players*: Frank

Sinatra, Jay Black, Verna Bloom, Martin Balsam, Joe DeSantis, Martin Gabel, Harry Guardino

THE FIRST DEADLY SIN (1980)
Filmways/Artanis/Cinema Seven: 101 minutes
Producers: George Pappas & Mark Shanker. *Director*: Brian G. Hutton. Screenplay by Mann Rubin. Based on the novel by Lawrence Sanders. *Photography (Color by TVC)*: Jack Priestley. Music by Gordon Jenkins. *Leading players*: Frank Sinatra, Faye Dunaway, David Dukes, George Coe, Brenda Vaccaro, Martin Gabel, Anthony Zerbe, James Whitmore, Joe Spinnell

CANNONBALL RUN II (1984)
Warner Brothers: 108 minutes
Producer: Albert S. Ruddy. *Director*: Hal Needham. *Screenplay*: Hal Needham, Albert S. Ruddy and Harvey Miller. Based on characters created by Brock Yates. *Photography (Technicolor)*: Nick McLean. *Music*: Al Capps. *Leading players*: Burt Reynolds, Dom DeLuise, Dean Martin, Sammy Davis Jun., Jamie Farr, Marilu Henner, Telly Savalas, Shirley MacLaine, Frank Sinatra (as himself)

WHO FRAMED ROGER RABBIT (1988)
Touchstone, Amblin/Warner Brothers: 104 minutes
Producers: Robert Watts & Frank Marshall. *Director*: Robert Zemeckis. Screenplay by Jeffrey Price & Peter S. Seaman. Based on the novel *Who Censored Roger Rabbit?* by Gary K. Wolf. *Photography (in colour)*: Dean Cundey. Music by Alan Silvestri. *Leading players*: Bob Hoskins, Christopher Lloyd, Joanna Cassidy, Stubby Kaye, Alan Tilvern. Sinatra featured as the voice of the cartoon character 'Singing Sword'

Discography

Sinatra began recording his first albums for Capitol in 1953. The following list comprises the highlights of the LPs he has released in the subsequent forty years, first for Capitol and then for his own company Reprise. Film songs (including many of those mentioned in the text and credits of this book) feature prominently in the albums. One LP, *Sinatra Sings Of Days Of Wine and Roses*, is devoted entirely to movie songs. Others include such rarities as the theme song from *Not As A Stranger*, 'Monique', the theme from *Kings Go Forth*, 'Soliloquy' which he so very nearly sang on screen in *Carousel*, and even 'I Like To Lead When I Dance' which, despite Sammy Cahn's lamentations, Sinatra did record as part of the *Sinatra 65* album, a year after the release of *Robin And The Seven Hoods*.

The list begins with the first Capitol release *Swing Easy* and concludes with his latest album, *Duets*. Compilation LPs, reissues, Greatest Hits, etc. are not included as the list is devoted primarily to albums with original recordings.

The albums released by Columbia and RCA are composed of singles (recorded by Sinatra between 1939 and 1952) that were subsequently gathered together and released as albums. For the record they are as follows: *The Dorsey/Sinatra Sessions 1940–42*, a six-LP set released by RCA Victor; *Sinatra Plus*, a Fontana double album devoted to the years 1939–52; *The Essential Frank Sinatra*, a three-LP set from CBS, again covering the years 1939–52; *In The Beginning, Frank Sinatra*, a CBS double album

167

devoted to 1943–51 and *Sinatra Souvenir*, a Sinatra album from Fontana covering the six years, 1944–50.

The Capitol Years

SWING EASY (1953)
Arranger: Nelson Riddle
Just One Of Those Things; I'm Gonna Sit Right Down and Write Myself a Letter; Sunday; Wrap Your Troubles In Dreams; Taking a Chance on Love; Jeepers Creepers; Get Happy; All Of Me

SONGS FOR YOUNG LOVERS (1954)
Arrangers: Nelson Riddle & George Siravo
My Funny Valentine; The Girl Next Door; A Foggy Day; Like Someone in Love; I Get A Kick Out of You; Little Girl Blue; They Can't Take That Away from Me; Violets for Your Furs

IN THE WEE SMALL HOURS (1955)
Arranger: Nelson Riddle
In the Wee Small Hours of the Morning; Mood Indigo; Glad to Be Unhappy; I Get Along Without You Very Well; Deep in a Dream; I See Your Face Before Me; Can't We Be Friends; When Your Lover Has Gone; What Is This Thing Called Love; Last Night When We Were Young; I'll Be Around; Ill Wind; It Never Entered My Mind; Dancing On The Ceiling; I'll Never Be The Same; This Love of Mine (co-written by Sinatra)

SONGS FOR SWINGIN' LOVERS (1956)
Arranger: Nelson Riddle
You Make Me Feel So Young; It Happened in Monterey; You're Getting to be a Habit with Me; You Brought a New Kind of Love to Me; Too Marvellous for Words; Old Devil Moon; Pennies from Heaven; Love is Here to Stay; I've Got You Under My Skin; I Thought About You; We'll Be Together Again; Makin' Whoopee; Swingin' Down The Lane; Anything Goes; How About You

HIGH SOCIETY (1956)
Soundtrack of MGM movie
High Society Calypso; Little One; Who Wants To Be a Millionaire?; True Love; You're Sensational; I Love You Samantha; Now You Has Jazz; Well Did You Evah?; Mind If I Make Love To You

THIS IS SINATRA (1957)
Arranger: Nelson Riddle
I've Got the World on a String; Three Coins In The Fountain; Love and Marriage; From Here to Eternity; South of the Border; Rain (Falling From The Skies); The Gal That Got Away; Young at Heart; Learnin' the Blues; My One and Only Love; The Tender Trap; Don't Worry 'Bout Me

CLOSE TO YOU (1957)
Arranger: Nelson Riddle
Close To You; P.S. I Love You; Love Locked Out; Everything Happens to Me; It's Easy to Remember; Don't Like Goodbyes; With Every Breath I Take; Blame It on My Youth; It Could Happen to You; I've Had My Moments; I Couldn't Sleep A Wink Last Night; The End of a Love Affair

A SWINGIN' AFFAIR (1957)
Arranger: Nelson Riddle
Night And Day; I Wish I Were in Love Again; No One Ever Tells You; I Got Plenty O' Nuttin'; I Guess I'll Have to Change My Plan; Nice Work if You Can Get it; Stars Fell on Alabama; I Won't Dance; The Lonesome Road; At Long Last Love; You'd Be So Nice to Come Home To; I Got It Bad and That Ain't Good; From This Moment On; If I Had You; Oh! Look at Me Now

PAL JOEY (1957)
Soundtrack of Columbia movie
There's a Small Hotel; Bewitched; Do It the Hard Way; Plant You Now, Dig You Later; You Mustn't Kick It Around; That Terrific Rainbow; I Didn't Know What Time It Was; The Lady Is a Tramp; Strip Number; Dream Sequence; My Funny Valentine; I Could Write a Book; Main Title; Great Big Town; Zip

WHERE ARE YOU? (1958)
Arranger: Gordon Jenkins
Where Are You?; The Night We Called it a Day; I Cover The Waterfront; Maybe You'll Be There; Laura; Lonely Town; Autumn Leaves; I'm a Fool To Want You (co-written by Sinatra); I Think of You; Where Is the One; There's No You; Baby, Won't You Please Come Home

169

COME FLY WITH ME (1958)
Arranger: Billy May
Come Fly With Me; Around The World; Isle of Capri; Moonlight in Vermont; Autumn in New York; On The Road to Mandalay; Let's Get Away from It all; April In Paris; London by Night; Brazil; Blue Hawaii; It's Nice to Go Trav'ling ... But It's Oh So Nice to Come Home

THIS IS SINATRA VOL 2 (1958)
Arranger: Nelson Riddle
Hey! Jealous Lover; Everybody Loves Somebody; Something Wonderful Happens in Summer; Half as Lovely Twice as True; You're Cheating Yourself; You'll Always Be The One I Love; You Forgot All The Words; How Little We Know; Time After Time; Crazy Love; Wait for Me; If You Are but a Dream; So Long, My Love; It's the Same Old Dream; I Believe; Put Your Dreams Away

FRANK SINATRA SINGS FOR ONLY THE LONELY (1958)
Arranger: Nelson Riddle
Only The Lonely; Angel Eyes; What's New; It's a Lonesome Old Town; Willow Weep for Me; Goodbye; Blues in the Night; Guess I'll Hang My Tears Out to Dry; Ebb Tide; Spring Is Here; Gone With The Wind; One for My Baby

COME DANCE WITH ME (1959)
Arrangers: Billy May and Heinie Beau
Come Dance With Me; Something's Gotta Give; Just in Time; Dancing in the Dark; Too Close for Comfort; I Could Have Danced All Night; Saturday Night; Day In–Day Out; Cheek to Cheek; Baubles, Bangles and Beads; The Song Is You; The Last Dance'

LOOK TO YOUR HEART (1959)
Arranger: Nelson Riddle
Look to Your Heart; Anytime, Anywhere; When I Stop Loving You; Not As A Stranger; Our Town; You, my Love; Same old Saturday Night; Fairy Tale; The Impatient Years; I Could Have Told You; If I Had Three Wishes; I'm Gonna Live Till I Die

NO ONE CARES (1959)
Arranger: Gordon Jenkins
When No One Cares; A Cottage For Sale; Stormy Weather; Where Do You Go; I Don't Stand a Ghost of a Chance With You; Here's That Rainy Day; I Can't Get Started; Why Try to Change Me Now; Just Friends; I'll Never Smile Again; None but the Lonely Heart

CAN-CAN (1960)
Soundtrack of 20th Century-Fox movie
Entr'acte; It's All Right With Me; Come Along With Me; Live and Let Live; You Do Something to Me; Let's Do It; I Love Paris; Montmartre; C'est Magnifique; Can-Can; It Was Just One of Those Things

NICE 'N' EASY (1960)
Arranger: Nelson Riddle
'Nice 'N' Easy; That Old Feeling; How Deep Is the Ocean; I've Got a Crush on You; You Go to My Head; Fools Rush In; Nevertheless; She's Funny That Way; Try a Little Tenderness; Embraceable You; Mam'selle; Dream

SINATRA'S SWINGIN' SESSION (1960)
Arranger: Nelson Riddle
When You're Smiling; Blue Moon; S'posin'; It All Depends on You; It's Only a Paper Moon; My Blue Heaven; Should I; September In The Rain; Always; I Can't Believe That You're In Love with Me; I Concentrate on You; You Do Something to Me

ALL THE WAY (1960)
Arranger: Nelson Riddle
All The Way; High Hopes; Talk to Me; French Foreign Legion; To Love and Be Loved; River, Stay Away From My Door; Witchcraft; It's Over, It's Over, It's Over; Ol' MacDonald (Had a Farm); This Was My Love; All My Tomorrows

COME SWING WITH ME! (1961)
Arrangers: Billy May and Heinie Beau
Day By Day; Sentimental Journey; Almost Like Being in Love; Five Minutes More; American Beauty Rose; Yes Indeed!; On The Sunny Side Of The Street; Don't Take Your Love From Me; That Old Black Magic; Lover; Paper Doll; I've Heard That Song Before

SINATRA SINGS ... OF LOVE AND THINGS! (1962)
Arrangers: Nelson Riddle, Felix Slatkin & Skip Martin
The Nearness of You; Hidden Persuasion; The Moon Was Yellow; I Love Paris; Monique; Chicago; Love Looks So Well On You; Sentimental Baby; Mister Success; They Came to Cordura; I Gotta Right To Sing The Blues; Something Wonderful Happens In Summer

171

POINT OF NO RETURN (1962)
Arranger: Axel Stordahl
When The World Was Young; I'll Remember April; September Song; A Million Dreams Ago; I'll See You Again; There Will Never Be Another You; Somewhere Along The Way; It's a Blue World; These Foolish Things; As Time Goes By; I'll Be Seeing You; Memories of You

The Reprise Years

RING-A-DING DING! (1961)
Arranger: Johnny Mandel
Ring-a-ding ding!; Let's Fall in Love; Be Careful, It's My Heart; A Foggy Day; A Fine Romance; In The Still Of The Night; The Coffee Song; When I Take My Sugar To Tea; Let's Face The Music And Dance; You'd Be So Easy To Love; You And The Night And The Music; I've Got My Love To Keep Me Warm

SINATRA SWINGS (1962)
Arranger: Billy May
Falling In Love; The Curse Of An Aching Heart; Don't Cry Joe; Please Don't Talk About Me When I'm Gone; Love Walked In; Granada; I Never Knew; Don't Be That Way; Moonlight On The Ganges; It's a Wonderful World; Have You Met Miss Jones?; You're Nobody Till Somebody Loves You

I REMEMBER TOMMY (1962)
Arranger: Sy Oliver
I'm Getting Sentimental Over You; Imagination; There Are Such Things; East Of The Sun; Daybreak; Without A Song; I'll Be Seeing You; Take Me; It's Always You; Polka Dots and Moonbeams; It Started All Over Again; The One I Love (Belongs to Somebody Else)

SINATRA AND STRINGS (1962)
Arranger: Don Costa
I Hadn't Anyone Till You; Night And Day; Misty; Stardust; Come Rain or Shine; It Might As Well Be Spring; Prisoner of Love; That's All; All or Nothing At all; Yesterdays

SINATRA AND SWINGIN' BRASS (1962)
Arranger: Neal Hefti
Goody Goody; They Can't Take That Away From Me; At Long Last

Love; I'm Beginning To See The Light; Don'cha Go 'way Mad; I Get A Kick Out Of You; Tangerine; Love Is Just Around the Corner; Ain't She Sweet; Serenade In Blue; I Love You; Pick Yourself Up

SINATRA SINGS GREAT SONGS FROM GREAT BRITAIN (1962)
Arranger: Robert Farnon
The Very Thought Of You; We'll Gather Lilacs; If I Had You; Now Is The Hour; The Gipsy; A Nightingale Sang in Berkeley Square; A Garden In The Rain; London By Night; We'll Meet Again; I'll Follow My Secret Heart

ALL ALONE (1962)
Arranger: Gordon Jenkins
All Alone; The Girl Next Door; Are You Lonesome Tonight?; Charmaine; What'll I Do?; When I Lost You; Oh, How I Miss You Tonight; Indiscreet (title song); You Forgot To Remember; Together; The Song Is Ended

SINATRA AND BASIE (1963)
Arranger: Neal Hefti
Pennies from Heaven; Please Be Kind; The Tender Trap; Looking At The World Through Rose-Coloured Glasses; My Kind of Gal; I Only Have Eyes For You; Nice Work If You Can Get it; Learnin' The Blues; I'm Gonna Sit Right Down and Write Myself a Letter; I Won't Dance

THE CONCERT SINATRA (1963)
Arranger: Nelson Riddle
I Have Dreamed; My Heart Stood Still; Lost In The Stars; Ol' Man River; You'll Never Walk Alone; Bewitched; This Nearly Was Mine; Soliloquy

SINATRA'S SINATRA (1963)
Arranger: Nelson Riddle
I've Got You Under My Skin; In The Wee Small Hours Of The Morning; The Second Time Around; Nancy; Witchcraft; Young At Heart; All The Way; How Little We Know; Pocketful of Miracles; Oh, What It Seemed To Be; Call Me Irresponsible; Put Your Dreams Away

FRANK SINATRA SINGS DAYS OF WINE AND ROSES, MOON RIVER AND OTHER ACADEMY AWARD WINNERS (1964)
Arranger: Nelson Riddle

173

Days Of Wine And Roses; Moon River; The Way You Look Tonight; Three Coins In The Fountain; In The Cool, Cool, Cool of the Evening; Secret Love; Swinging on a Star; It Might As Well Be Spring; The Continental; Love Is A Many Splendoured Thing; All The Way

IT MIGHT AS WELL BE SWING (1964)
Arranger: Quincy Jones
Fly Me To The Moon; I Wish You Love; I Believe In You; More; I Can't Stop Loving You; Hello Dolly; I Wanna Be Around; The Best is Yet To Come; The Good Life; Wives And Lovers

SOFTLY AS I LEAVE YOU (1964)
Arrangers: Ernie Freeman, Nelson Riddle and Billy May
Emily; Here's to the Losers; Dear Heart; Come Blow Your Horn; Love Isn't Just For The Young; I Can't Believe I'm Losing You; Pass Me By; Softly As I Leave You; Then Suddenly Love; Available; Talk to me Baby; The Look of Love

SEPTEMBER OF MY YEARS (1965)
Arranger: Gordon Jenkins
The September of My Years; How Old Am I?; Don't Wait Too Long; It Gets Lonely Early; This Is All I Ask; Last Night When We Were Young; The Man In The Looking Glass; It Was A Very Good Year; When The Wind Was Green; Hello Young Lovers; I See It Now; Once Upon A Time; September Song

SINATRA '65 (1965)
Arranger: Nelson Riddle
Tell Her (You Love Her Each Day); Anytime At All; The Cardinal (title number); I Like To Lead When I Dance; You Brought A New Kind Of Love To Me; My Kind Of Town; When Somebody Loves You; Somewhere In Your Heart; I've Never Been In Love Before; When I'm Not Near The Girl I Love; Luck Be A Lady To Me

MY KIND OF BROADWAY (1965)
Arrangers: Billy May, Nelson Riddle and Torrie Zito
Everybody Has The Right To Be Wrong; Golden Moments; Luck Be A Lady; Lost In The Stars; Hello Dolly!; I'll Only Miss Her When I Think Of Her; They Can't Take That Away From Me; Yesterdays; Nice Work If You Can Get It; Have You Met Miss Jones?; Without a Song

A MAN AND HIS MUSIC (1965)
Double album, narrated and sung by Sinatra
Arrangers: Nelson Riddle, Gordon Jenkins, Billy May, Sy Oliver, Don Costa, Johnny Mandel, Ernie Freeman
Album One: Put Your Dreams Away; All Or Nothing At All; I'll Never Smile Again; There Are Such Things; I'll Be Seeing You; The One I Love Belongs To Somebody Else; Polka Dots and Moonbeams; Night And Day; Oh, What It Seemed To Be; Soliloquy; Nancy; The House I Live In; From Here To Eternity (extract from film with Sinatra and Montgomery Clift)
Album Two: Come Fly With Me; How Little We Know; Learnin' The Blues; In The Wee Small Hours Of The Morning; Young At Heart; Witchcraft; All The Way; Love and Marriage; I've Got You Under My Skin; Ring-a-ding ding!; The Second Time Around; The Summit (comedy routine with Sinatra, Dean Martin and Sammy Davis Jun.); The Oldest Established (permanent floating crap game) – with Bing Crosby and Dean Martin; Luck Be A Lady; Call Me Irresponsible; Fly Me To The Moon; Softly As I Leave You; My Kind Of Town; The September Of My Years

STRANGERS IN THE NIGHT (1966)
Arrangers: Ernie Freeman and Nelson Riddle
Strangers In The Night; Summer Wind; All Or Nothing At All; Call Me; You're Driving Me Crazy; On A Clear Day; My Baby Just Cares For Me; Down Town; Yes Sir, That's My Baby; The Most Beautiful Girl In The World

MOONLIGHT SINATRA (1966)
Arranger: Nelson Riddle
Moonlight Becomes You; Moon Song; Moonlight Serenade; Reaching For The Moon; I Wished On The Moon; Oh You Crazy Moon; The Moon Got In My Eyes; Moonlight Mood; Moon Love; The Moon Was Yellow

SINATRA AT THE SANDS (1966)
Arrangers: Quincy Jones and Billy Byers
Double album: Come Fly With Me; I've Got A Crush On You; I've Got You Under My Skin; The Shadow Of Your Smile; Street of Dreams; One For My Baby; Fly Me To The Moon; One O'Clock Jump; (Frank Sinatra monologue); You Make Me Feel So Young; All Of Me; The September of My Years; Get Me To The Church On Time; It Was A Very Good Year; Don't Worry 'Bout Me; Makin' Whoopee; Where or When; Angel Eyes; My Kind Of Town; (Sinatra

closing monologue); My Kind Of Town

THAT'S LIFE (1966)
Arranger: Ernie Freeman
That's Life; I Will Wait For You; Somewhere My Love; Sand And Sea; What Now My Love; Winchester Cathedral; Give Her Love; Tell Her; Impossible Dream; You're Gonna Hear From Me

FRANCIS ALBERT SINATRA & ANTONIO CARLOS JOBIM (1967)
Arranger: Claus Ogerman
The Girl From Ipanema; Dindi; Change Partners; Quiet Nights of Quiet Stars; Meditation; If You Never Come To Me; How Insensitive; I Concentrate On You; Baubles, Bangles and Beads; Once I Loved

FRANK SINATRA AND THE WORLD WE KNEW (1967)
Arrangers: Billy Strange, Gordon Jenkins, Ernie Freeman and H.B. Barnun
The World We Knew; Somethin' Stupid (with Nancy Sinatra); This Is My Love; Born Free; Don't Sleep In The Subway; This Town; This Is My Song; You Are There; Drinking Again; Some Enchanted Evening

FRANCIS A. AND EDWARD K. (1968)
Arranger: Billy May
Follow Me; Sunny; All I Need Is The Girl; Indian Summer; I Like The Sunrise; Yellow Days; Poor Butterfly; Come Back To Me

CYCLES (1968)
Arranger: Don Costa
Rain In My Heart; From Both Sides Now; Little Green Apples; Pretty Colours; Cycles; Wandering; By The Time I Get To Phoenix; Moody River; My Way Of Life; Gentle On My Mind

MY WAY (1969)
Arranger: Don Costa
Watch What Happens; Didn't We?; Hallelujah; I Love Her So; Yesterday; All My Tomorrows; My Way; A Day In The Life of a Fool; For Once In My Life; If You Go Away; Mrs Robinson

A MAN ALONE (1969)
Arranger: Don Costa
A Man Alone; Night; I've Been To Town; From Promise to Promise; The Single Man; The Beautiful Strangers; Lonesome Cities; Love's

Been Good To Me; Empty Is; Out Beyond The Window; Some Travelling Music; A Man Alone

WATERTOWN (1969)
Arrangers: Bob Gaudio, Charles Callelo and Joe Scott
Watertown; Goodbye; For a While; Michael and Peter; I Would Be In Love; Elizabeth; What A Funny Girl; What's Now Is Now; She Says; The Train

SINATRA AND COMPANY (1970)
Arrangers: Eumir Deodato and Don Costa
Drinking Water; Someone To Light Up My Life; Triste; Don't Ever Go Away; This Happy Madness; Wave; One Note Samba; I Will Drink The Wine; Close To You; Sunrise In The Morning; Bein' Green; My Sweet Lady; Leaving On A Jet Plane; Lady Day

OL' BLUE EYES IS BACK (1973)
Arrangers: Gordon Jenkins and Don Costa
You Will Be My Music; You're So Right; Winners; Nobody Wins; Send In The Clowns; Dream Away; Let Me Try Again; There Used To Be A Ball Park; Noah

SOME NICE THINGS I'VE MISSED (1974)
Arrangers: Don Costa and Gordon Jenkins
You Turned My World Around; Sweet Caroline; The Summer Knows; If; You Are The Sunshine Of My Life; What Are You Doing The Rest Of Your Life?; I'm Gonna Make It All The Way; Tie A Yellow Ribbon Round The Ole Oak Tree; Satisfy Me; One More Time; Bad, bad Leroy Brown

SINATRA – THE MAIN EVENT (1974)
With Woody Herman in concert
The Lady Is A Tramp; I Get A Kick Out Of You; Let Me Try Again; Autumn In New York; I've Got You Under My Skin; Bad, bad Leroy Brown; Angel Eyes; You Are The Sunshine Of My Life; The House I Live In; My Kind Of Town; My Way

TRILOGY (PAST, PRESENT, FUTURE) (1980)
Three Album Set
Record 1: Arranger: Billy May
The Song Is You; But Not For Me; I Had The Craziest Dream; It Had To Be You; Let's Face The Music And Dance; Street Of Dreams; My Shining Hour; All Of You; More Than You Know; They All Laughed

Record 2: Arranger: Don Costa
You And Me; Just The Way You Are; Something: MacArthur Park;
Theme from New York, New York; Summer Me, Winter Me; Song
Sung Blue; For The Good Times; Love Me Tender; That's What
God Looks Like
Record 3: The Future, a musical fantasy in three tenses, composed,
arranged and conducted by Gordon Jenkins, with the Philharmonic
Symphony Orchestra and Chorus. What Time Does The Next
Miracle Leave; World War None!; The Future; Before The Music
Ends

SHE SHOT ME DOWN (1981)
Arrangers: Gordon Jenkins, Don Costa and Nelson Riddle
Good Things Going; Hey Look, No Crying; Thanks For The
Memory; A Long Night; Bang Bang (My Baby Shot Me Down);
Monday Morning Quarterback; South – To A Warmer Place; I Loved
Her; The Gal That Got Away/It Never Entered My Mind (medley)

L.A. IS MY LADY (1984)
Produced and conducted by Quincy Jones
L.A. Is My Lady; The Best Of Everything; How Do You Keep The
Music Playing; Teach Me Tonight; It's All Right With Me; Mack The
Knife; Until The Real Thing Comes Along; Stormy Weather; If I
Should Lose You; A Hundred Years From Today; After You've Gone

Capitol

DUETS (1993)
Conductor and musical director: Patrick Williams
The Lady Is A Tramp (with Luther Vandross); What Now My Love
(with Aretha Franklin); I've Got A Crush On You (with Barbra
Streisand); Summer Wind (with Julio Iglesias); Come Rain or Come
Shine (with Gloria Estefan); New York, New York (with Tony
Bennett); They Can't Take That Away From Me (with Natalie Cole);
You Make Me Feel So Young (with Charles Aznavour); Guess I'll
Hang My Tears Out To Dry/In The Wee Small Hours Of The
Morning (with Carly Simon); I've Got The World On A String (with
Liza Minnelli); Witchcraft (with Anita Baker); I've Got You Under My
Skin (with Bono); All The Way/One For My Baby (with Kenny G)

Sinatra on Video

Several videos of Sinatra in concert and of his TV Specials have been released in recent years. The following are among the most rewarding:

A Man And His Music (TV Special, 1965)
A Man And His Music II (TV Special, 1966)
A Man And His Music + Ella + Jobim (TV Special, 1967)
Sinatra In Concert: Royal Festival Hall, 1970
The Main Event: Frank Sinatra In Concert: Madison Square Garden, 1974
Sinatra and Friends (TV Special, 1977)
The First 40 Years (TV Special, 1979)
A Man And His Music with Count Basie (TV Special, 1981)
Sinatra Concert For The Americas from Santo Domingo; 1982
Sinatra in Japan, 1985
Frank Sinatra: Portrait Of An Album with Quincy Jones and his Orchestra, 1985

Bibliography

Capra, Frank, *The Name Above The Title: An Autobiography* (Macmillan, New York, 1971)

Douglas-Home, Robin, *Sinatra* (Michael Joseph, London, 1962)

Gardner, Ava, *Ava: My Story* (Bantam Books, New York, 1990)

Higham, Charles & Greenberg, Joel, *The Celluloid Muse* (Angus & Robertson, London, 1969)

Hodge, Jessica, *Frank Sinatra* (Magna Books, Leicester, 1992)

Hotchner, A.E., *Doris Day: Her Own Story* (W.H. Allen, London, 1976)

Jewell, Derek, *Frank Sinatra: A Celebration* (Pavilion Books, London, 1985)

Kazan, Elia, *Elia Kazan: A Life* (Alfred A. Knopf, New York, 1988)

Kelley, Kitty, *His Way* (Bantam Press, New York, 1986)

Minnelli, Vincente (with Hector Acre), *I Remember It Well* (Doubleday, New York, 1974)

Peters, Richard, *The Frank Sinatra Scrapbook* (Pop Universal/Souvenir Press, London, 1982)

Pratley, Gerald, *The Cinema of John Frankenheimer* (A. Zwemmer, London, 1969)

Preminger, Otto, *Preminger: An Autobiography* (Doubleday, New York, 1977)

Ringgold, Gene & McCarthy, Clifford, *The Films of Frank Sinatra* (Citadel, New Jersey, 1971)

Rockwell, John, *Sinatra: An American Classic* (Elm Tree Books, London, 1984)

Shaw, Arnold, *Sinatra: A Biography* (W.H. Allen, London 1968)

Sinatra, Nancy, *Frank Sinatra: My Father* (Hodder and Stoughton, London, 1985)

Thomas, Bob, *Brando: Portrait of the Rebel as an Artist* (W.H. Allen, London, 1973)

Thomas, Bob, *Clown Prince Of Hollywood: The Antic Life And Times of Jack L. Warner* (McGraw-Hill, New York, 1990)
Thomas, Bob, *King Cohn* (Barrie and Rockliff, London, 1967)

Index